FINDING YOUR KICK-ASS BUTTON

TURNING PAIN INTO POWER

KICK-ASS BUTTON

FINDING YOUR KICK-ASS BUTTON

TURNING PAIN INTO POWER

GIN CLIFTON

MUNN
AVENUE
PRESS

FINDING YOUR KICK-ASS BUTTON
TURNING PAIN INTO POWER
By Gin Clifton

First Edition
Copyright © 2024 by Virginia Clifton

Published by
Munn Avenue Press
300 Main Street, Ste 21
Madison, NJ 07940
MunnAvenuePress.com

This book is a memoir. It reflects the author's present recollections of experiences over time. Some names and characteristics have been changed, some events have been compressed, and some dialogue has been recreated.

For permission requests, contact MunnAvenuePress.com

Paperback ISBN# 978-1-960299-58-1
Hardcover ISBN# 978-1-960299-59-8
Printed in the United States of America

Thank you to my Mother for giving me the gift of life.
It's a blessing to be alive.

Thank you to my children for giving me purpose and for showing
me what unconditional love feels like.

Thank you to my Granny for loving me and believing
in me always.

My Aunt, My Rock—you are a rare breed! I was never a burden
or too much for you, even in my darkest hour. Thank you for
giving me never ending love.

A big thank you to special people in my community who
continue to help me, comfort me, and include me in gatherings
which has allowed my kids to feel a sense of belonging within
their community, even after divorce.

Kris, thank you for helping me jump start my career after
a long absence and believing in me. The gift of employment
allowed me to begin this journey towards becoming the
best version of myself.

Thank you to my family and friends who cheered me on
when I had a crazy dream to change my life, fight my demons,
and write a book.

To the young teenage moms who are doing their best—
I recognize you!

To the selfless volunteers who work hard so the world can
be a better place, I recognize you!

To those who suffer from abuse—I hug you.

CONTENTS

– 1 –

GERMAN BEGINNINGS

No one knew of the abuse. From the outside looking in, the portrait of our family was one to behold: the alluring couple, the three well-mannered children; our lives appeared to be woven from threads of joy and social grace. Within the tight-knit community of Würzburg, Germany, where we lived off-post when my dad wasn't stationed on a military base, my parents shimmered with sociability. My father rose through the ranks to grand master of the local Masonic lodge, and both were active in the Eastern Star. Our social calendar was punctuated with events, the lodge acting as the heartbeat of our gatherings—from wedding receptions to festive Christmas parties.

In Würzburg, we lived in a house with lots of cascading fruit trees that were heavy with apples and cherries in the late summer days. The backyard had an empty swimming pool that my dad filled to the top with tree trimmings, branches, and other brambles. It was on a large acre or two, vast and peaceful. I have a picture of me riding my bike on the overgrown pathway. There was a magical, yet melancholy feel to the landscape, as if the trees and the underbrush held the sorrow and unrest in their bowing limbs before we even fully knew it ourselves.

We lived on the army base in Schweinfurt for a few years. Our last tour, or placement there, was when we lived above the dentist's office—more specifically, in a suburb called Niederwerrn. In this close-knit community, bonds were forged, and my parents often extended their conviviality beyond the formalities of organized gatherings.

My father, with his knack for conversation and a jokester's gleam in his eye, was a magnet of likability. His humor, a curious mix of charm and mischief, won hearts with ease.

He was a teacher of impish lessons, once encouraging my young fingers to flick an ill-timed salute—a game that reached its abrupt end with his boss on the receiving end. He orchestrated beneath-the-covers antics, sealing us in before unleashing a thunderous fart. And, of course, the classic pull-my-finger ruse was a staple in his repertoire of pranks, much to our innocent delight.

My contributions to the family economy began with the polishing of his military boots, a task that filled me with a sense of purpose for a quarter's reward, a child's fortune. I remember a mishap at Burger King, where my clumsy fingers led to a ketchup explosion upon his shirt, painting his surprise in vivid red—a momentary lapse into the realm of the comical in our carefully curated lives. Playful tussles, impromptu karate chops, and games of mercy were commonplace in our household, a rollicking dance of mock combat and laughter. Our family game nights were spirited contests of strategy and luck, where Connect Four, Risk, and Checkers ruled, though the notorious 52-card pickup was the least of our favorites.

Wrestling matches flickered on our television, igniting our own versions of the sport as we mimicked the moves of the giants on the screen. And throughout it all, I was his Ginny Poo Snicky, the moniker he bestowed that carried the weight of affectionate jest. We were his "little squirts," a term of endearment that, despite its casual tone, bore the mark of a familial bond that defied the challenges we faced.

ONE NIGHT IN LATE OCTOBER, when the air was crisp with the promise of autumn and the streets were lined with jack-o'-lanterns and fake cobwebs, my dad was on overnight duty on the post, a routine shift that usually passed without incident. But this night was different. The call came in sometime after midnight. At first, I thought nothing of it as my dad often got calls during his shifts. But when he came home the next morning, his face was a mix of anger and concern that I'd rarely seen before.

"You won't believe what happened last night," he said, shaking his head as he sat down at the kitchen table.

My mom and I leaned in, curious. That's when he told us about the call he'd received. Some soldiers, probably bored and definitely cruel, had decided to "have some fun" with a stray cat they'd found wandering around the base. They burned its whiskers and laughed as the poor creature squirmed in pain and fear.

I remember feeling sick to my stomach as my dad recounted the story. But then his expression softened a bit. "I couldn't just leave her there," he said.

That's when I noticed the small pet carrier by his feet. Inside was a scrawny brown and black tabby cat with white paws, her eyes wide with fear but her whiskers mercifully intact. Dad had intervened before any serious harm was done.

"The soldiers are facing disciplinary action," he explained. "Extra duty, chores, the works. But I couldn't let this little one stay on base after what happened."

Mom and I exchanged glances. We both knew what was coming next.

"Can we keep her?" I asked, already falling in love with the tiny ball of fur.

Dad smiled, the first real smile since he'd walked in the door. "I thought you'd never ask."

We spent the rest of the morning getting the cat settled in, making a cozy bed out of old blankets, and finding a makeshift litter box. As she started to relax, purring softly as I stroked her head, the question of her name came up.

"Well," Mom said, looking at the calendar, "It's almost Halloween. How about Pumpkin?"

And just like that, Pumpkin became a part of our family. She was a reminder that even in the darkest moments, there's always a chance for rescue, for kindness, for a new beginning. Every time I saw her, I was proud of my dad for stepping in, and for showing compassion when others had shown cruelty.

Pumpkin lived with us for many years, a constant presence through moves and life changes. And every October, as the pumpkins appeared on porches and the leaves turned golden, we'd remember the night she came into our lives—a tiny multi-colored beacon of hope in the autumn darkness.

I'll never forget my dad's unique approach to conflict resolution. When my siblings and I would get into one of our epic arguments—you know, the kind that starts over something trivial like who got the last cookie and somehow escalates into a full-blown shouting match—Dad would step in with his unconventional peacekeeping method.

He'd disappear into his room for a moment and we'd all freeze, wondering what was coming. Then he'd emerge with one of his big, worn work shirts in hand and a mischievous glint in his eye. "Alright, you two," he'd say to whoever the main combatants were that day. "If you want to act like you're stuck together, then you're gonna be stuck together."

And just like that, he'd stuff us both into his shirt. Two squirming, grumbling kids were forced to share the same space inside a giant button-down. The shirt was always comically large on us, smelling of Dad's aftershave and that indefinable Dad scent.

"Now," he'd say, trying to keep a straight face, "you two are going to stay like that until you can figure out how to get along."

At first, we'd struggle against each other, trying to control where we were going. But pretty quickly, we'd realize that if we wanted to move at all, we had to work together. It's hard to stay mad at someone when you're literally stuck in the same shirt with them. We'd shuffle around the house like some sort of two-headed monster, bumping into furniture and giggling despite ourselves. The initial anger would fade, replaced by the ridiculousness of our situation. We'd start strategizing how to reach the TV remote or grab a snack from the kitchen, our earlier argument forgotten in the face of these new, shirt-based challenges.

Dad would watch us, pretending to go about his business but always with one eye on our progress. He'd wait until he saw the tension dissipate, until our frustrated grunts turned into laughter and cooperation.

"You two ready to be separate people again?" he'd ask after a while.

By that point, we usually were. The shirt would then come off and we'd be free again, our argument a distant memory. It was like magic, Dad's special brand of conflict resolution, wrapped up in an oversized cotton shirt. Ironic, coming from a man whose usual form of conflict resolution involved losing his temper and lashing out. But life was full of gray areas with my dad.

Looking back, I can see the genius of it. He was teaching us empathy, cooperation, and the art of letting go of petty disagreements, all without a single lecture. It's a lesson that stuck with me long after I outgrew his shirts.

I always knew when he was either going to blow or be reasonable. I could read his expressions and body language in a second and knew when I needed to retreat to my room because the shit was about to hit the fan. He was that guy who would beat the smithereens out of you and then take you to get ice cream afterward. When he was up, there was no one we would rather be with than him. And when he was down, he scared the living daylights out of us, and we would take cover.

Our lives were stitched together by a patchwork of German dwellings that were more affordable against the backdrop of a military-fueled economy. They enticed soldiers' families with extra allowances, a nudge to embrace life beyond the barracks. That's how we found ourselves perched above a dentist's practice in a three-bedroom abode, nestled in the heart of a bustling downtown, mere steps from the Edeka—a quaint store brimming with German delicacies.

I had a knack for looking like a German local, a skill I wore with pride. To this day, my mother might pass for a native speaker, necessity having sculpted her fluency.

School life was a shuttle dance between the base and the local institution, with buses shepherding us to our places of learning. My brother Mark, a high schooler then, embarked on a longer journey, his education lying at the end of an hour's ride while mine was a brief sprint away. Mark was four years older than me, and our sister Mary bridged the gap between us by two and a half years. We were a trio, a unit of three—the sum of our parents' biological legacy.

When these memories took root, I was eleven, dipping my toes into the fifth grade. Mornings unfurled with routine's quiet hum. At the end of the day, Mom, whose nickname was Bets, was not one for culinary fanfare and was pragmatic at the stove; dinner was a duty, not a dalliance. Our shopping orbits revolved strictly around the commissary; our parents were staunch in their American ways. Unlike them, I yearned to savor the world outside, to take in Europe with hungry eyes, a longing likely born from their very reluctance.

Relocations dotted our time in Germany, yet we remained tethered to my mother's workplace. She served the mess halls from behind the scenes, responsible for stocking the kitchens and cupboards of each one, orchestrating the sustenance of soldiers with practiced efficiency. Mom's labor spanned beyond morning to dusk; I remember her working the graveyard shifts when she wielded the pricing gun like a conductor's baton, marking the merchandise in a silent symphony before dawn called her back to motherhood.

I grew acquainted with responsibility prematurely. A latchkey kid by second grade, I returned home to a house devoid of parents, my lunch hour a solo affair. Occasionally, Mom's voice would guide me from the tape recorder, an auditory embrace in a still house.

The return from school signposted our next duty— chores. They loomed like daily mountains to scale before Dad's inspection. Mom often raced him home to assist in our domestic drill, her presence a buffer against the storm of his discontent. Our home was an exercise in precision, each room a testament to the order that Dad demanded. Mary was the steward of the kitchen; her dominion was over the dishes and countertops. Mark was the keeper of dust-free surfaces and clean floors. And I was the guardian of the bathrooms' shine. The expectation was clear: perfection before Dad's arrival or face the consequences—a sting from the belt for any task undone and loss of our whole week's allowance of five dollars.

Dad's military discipline was a thread woven through the fabric of our lives. His white-gloved inspections were tribunals where the smallest smudge could mean a world of hurt. He was a man of signals and wires, a master sergeant who tethered the bases of Germany with invisible threads of communication.

Words can bruise as deeply as leather, and it was his voice that often lashed at me, sowing seeds of doubt with proclamations of my supposed inadequacies. "You'll amount to nothing," he'd say, or "You're stupid; you'll be pregnant by sixteen," a litany of disparagement that echoed in the corners of my young mind.

The incident with the shower cord remains etched in memory. A twisted shower coil led to a parade of interrogations in the dining room where Dad commanded performance as judge and jury. Each denial from my siblings was met with the swift punishment of the belt, a repeated chorus of fear and pain. As it came to be my turn, dread pooled within me, magnified with each strike upon my siblings. His grip was an iron clasp as the belt descended on me, the first lashes sharp with pain that soon gave way to numbness. When the agony became too great, I would fall to my knees, hoping this would ease the blows. Sometimes it worked, though other times he would continue, the belt scorching my back instead.

The mystery of the damaged shower coil remained unsolved, but to quell the tide of his anger, I uttered a false confession. His fury increased with each subsequent strike, accusations of deceit interwoven with the punishment. I never knew who was to blame for the unraveling coils, but in that moment, I was the sacrificial lamb to his wrath, bearing the brunt of punishment and the sharp edge of his words.

PICTURE-PERFECT PRISONS

IN THE CLAMOR OF THE RUNNING WATER, our bathroom transformed into a confessional. It became a sanctum where my mother, with frantic urgency, unfurled her desperate schemes to us. Her words, a tapestry of fear and resolution, stitched together a plan that was as harrowing as it was surreal. To hear her speak of buying explosives with a fervor born of too many beatings, too much indignity, was to witness a woman pushed to the brink.

She told us tales of clandestine meetings with some men who would take care of Dad with explosives and explained in great detail what would happen and how we would finally be free. A course in survival, where the stakes were life and a semblance of peace was an education no child should receive.

The walls of that bathroom held secrets heavy with the scent of urgency and rebellion. I remember the stark contrast of those moments—her voice a strained whisper over the sound of water against the backdrop of a terror that had become as routine as the morning sun. She would lock eyes with us and, with the fierceness of a mother, convey a sense of hope that we would all escape from that hell and find peace on the other side of it.

I was led to believe that her intentions were to collect his life insurance money, move back to the States, and live a free life.

At the outset, it all seemed a bit off-kilter to me, the plan as she laid it out, though I was young, and the world was a puzzle I couldn't quite solve. Her words painted a picture of a brand-new chapter, promising an escape to a serene life in Alabama, just as my mom had always dreamed. But it didn't fully register, the gravity of her words lost in the wishful thinking of a child's mind. I couldn't grasp that her plan—to plant explosives in Dad's car, set to detonate on the way to his morning routine at physical therapy, known as physical training in the army—was anything beyond whispers of desperation.

In the wake of my father's beatings, her words were the promise of a savior. She was plotting our deliverance, our passage from the turmoil we knew to a peace she had etched in our hearts. The prospect of betraying my mother's trust never crossed my mind. To entertain such thoughts was to invite a fate worse than we had already endured. In the frozen soil of fear that our family was rooted in, she stood as the lone figure of revolt. To us, she was not just the bearer of too much information or the architect of a plot that spoke of desperation; she was our rock and we trusted her.

Did I ever think of warning my father? The question

itself seemed a cruel joke. To turn to the man who embodied the very essence of fear, whose very presence was a catalyst for our collective terror, was unthinkable. We were bound in our silence, a pact sealed by the common bond of survival. In those whispered confessions, where the fate of our family hung in the balance, we were swept up in the storm of her fierce desire to end our suffering—a desire as deep and vast as the ocean itself.

At twelve, the world unfolds in absolutes—good and bad, right and wrong, love and hate. Nuance is a language not yet learned, and the complexities of adult pain are a lexicon of shadows. When my mother, her voice thick with desperate resolve, spoke of making my father go away, my child's mind spun webs of confusion. To me, going away lacked the finality of death. It held the innocence of a temporary absence. I don't think my brain ever really comprehended the full reality of the situation. It seemed like I was walking through a dream. Was my father to leave on some prolonged journey, or were we to pack our bags for an unknown destination? The grim reality of her words danced just beyond my comprehension.

My father, for his part, was no bastion of fidelity. His transgressions weren't just rumors or hushed suspicions, they were as tangible as the daylight that filtered through our windows and as real as my mother's boss who shadowed him every day. Their indiscretions were a sickening rhythm to the backdrop of my sixth-grade year. She was also a soldier; she had short blonde hair and lots of acne scarring on her face. No one would have ever called her an attractive woman. My sister and I used to babysit her cats before my mother went away. We assumed their affair started after my mother went away because he used to come home with cat hair all over his military uniform and we knew she was the one with all the cats, so we named her Cat Lady.

And so, within the steamed mirrors and the relentless drip of the faucet, our story unfolded—a tale of a family driven to the edge, of a mother's love twisted into a weapon, and of us children who carried the weight of an adult world on our shoulders. The beatings, the plotting, and the unshakable fear all coalesced into a narrative that begged to be told and needed to be understood. Not just a record of pain, but as a testament to the indomitable will to forge a path out of darkness.

Dad's anger was as reliable as a badly set watch—erratic and guaranteed to go off at the worst times. His temper swung with the unpredictable gusts of a summer squall, and we, his reluctant sailors in the dinghy of domestic life, learned to ride the waves of his fury. My siblings and I memorized his pattern. It would start out with him quiet, then pacing, then calling for one or all of us, and then the questions started. If he didn't like our answers, he started getting animated. He would reword what we said to fit his cause and then we'd need to repeat it back to him. Sometimes, that meant having to repeat back to him, "Yes, Dad, I'm stupid because I didn't know that math problem." My father's beatings were as punctual as the most devout parishioner's Sunday service, leaving us in a state of perpetual penance.

Post-storm, we'd gather like veterans at a reunion, badges of honor in shades of purple and blue, the living room our foxhole. The bruises were mainly on our backs, legs, and butts. But sometimes our hands were bruised from trying to shield ourselves. There we'd compare the trophies of the latest tempest, each bruise a story, each flinch a memory. We ticked off the days on the family calendar with a mix of dread and dark humor, wondering if next time we could issue rain checks on the familial thunderbolts.

Dad was the self-appointed king of our little domestic kingdom, wielding his scepter of terror like a discount Voldemort. It was as if he knew his brand of tyranny had the shelf life of milk left out in the sun—destined to sour and push us out the door. Following the revelation of Mom's plan, his temper storms reached Category Five and swept through our lives like a hurricane with a personal vendetta.

There was a footlocker that lived in my brother's closet, a vault for food where my dad would banish all the snacks and anything at all good to eat, in bouts of dietary self-discipline—a tangible manifestation of his battle with both weight and scarcity. The lingering aroma of meals past was eradicated from the house before his return home, an odd ritual to ward off temptation.

I took to hiding small rations of cheese in my drawers. Despite my parents both being employed by the military establishment, food was scarce because it was controlled by my father. Secretly securing my own rations was the only way I could ward off the endless, gnawing hunger pangs.

OUR MOTHER'S PLAN FELL APART, you could say, the day after the Super Bowl in 1988. She had planned to hire two men to lay the trap in the headrest of his car, paying them with the insurance money that would follow. Yet fate played its hand through an undercover German agent who was trying to prevent the sale of explosives in Germany and from whom by chance the men attempted to purchase the incendiary materials they needed, and the arrest unfolded with a cold efficiency at her workplace. It was a patchwork of confusion on the day of her arrest as we didn't know what had happened.

Instructions from school on how to get home were jumbled, leaving us to our own devices. I remember Mrs. Jenkins, my sixth-grade teacher, offering a ride, but we declined, steeped in the stoicism that our family's trials had taught us. Our walk home was a silent procession, punctuated by the absence of the ones who were meant to protect us.

That night, and for the weeks that followed, we found shelter with the Smiths, our family friends and neighbors. My dad asked the Smiths to take us for a bit so he could take care of the logistics like finding lawyers. Our house stood empty while Dad grappled with the tempest Mom's absence had wrought. The Smith family's kindness was a lighthouse in our dark seas and our shelter in that tempest. They lived in American housing on the military post nearby. Their household and three daughters were a haven of warmth, care, and the gentle normalcy we so craved. My siblings and I lived with them for about five weeks after Mom's arrest.

With Laura Smith, the matriarch and bowling enthusiast, we found moments of reprieve in the alley's din and the crash of pins. It was there, amidst the strikes and spares, that the truth of our bruises was revealed, a wordless confession to her shocked silence. Laura took us to the bathroom at the bowling alley where she demanded we show her our bruises. Her response was swift and brought the Criminal Investigation Division (CID) to our classroom doors.

As a sixth grader, the betrayal stung with the acute pain of broken trust. To me, it was a secret pilfered and paraded, a private anguish made public without my consent. Yet, with the distance of years, I understand the necessity from which her actions were born. She, in her compassion, saw not the breaking of confidence, but the saving of lives. The intervention she summoned was not a violation, but a rescue—an act of grace that pulled us from the depths of our despair.

Despite being shielded from our father's wrath, we wanted to be home. What if the CID took our father too? What would happen to us? In that uncertain time, we children were adrift and our bearings were lost amid the silent currents of adult strife. Information was a commodity no one thought to share with us, leaving us to navigate the murky waters of confusion and fear.

When we eventually moved back home, my father was meticulous, a tyrant of correspondence. He ensured that not a single envelope slipped by unopened, his fingers deftly splitting the seal, his paranoia seeking confessions in every line. He read all the mail coming in and going out. He would read it aloud sometimes in front of us, including letters from our mother sent while she was in jail. I felt like letters from my mom should be private and not read out loud for everyone to hear. But Dad said Mom might be trying to use code language to tell us things, so that's why he needed to read every piece of mail.

With Mom gone and Dad explosive at every turn, my friend Alice was my lifeline. I wish we were still in touch, but you know how it goes. Some friendships are built on unspoken reciprocity—I'll take your kid for a sleepover, and you'll take mine next time. But with Alice, it was never that way. It was always me going to her place, and her family never seemed to mind.

I remember trying to have a friend over once. I've forgotten her name now, but I'll never forget how it went down. Dad started yelling, and the whole atmosphere just turned sour. After that, I never invited anyone over again. It was easier and safer to just be the guest.

Alice's house was different. They didn't live on the military post. Instead, they had a German house in a neighborhood with a mix of American and German families. It felt like a whole other world to me. She had a brother, and we'd all hang out together, blasting Salt-N-Pepa and other rap tunes, feeling like we were the coolest kids on the block.

I got pretty good at navigating the German bus system to get to her place. There I was, this American kid in sixth grade, confidently telling the bus driver my stop in broken German, dropping coins into the slot like I'd been doing it my whole life. The bus stop was right outside our high-rise in Schweinfurt, across from the PX, or post exchange. It felt like freedom, being able to just leave our apartment, hop on a bus, and escape to Alice's world.

Her house always felt different—warmer, somehow. We didn't spend a ton of time chatting with her parents, but they were always welcoming. There was always dinner, always a place for me. I was like another kid to them, really.

I think maybe God or the universe or whatever you believe in knew I needed that lifeline.

The weird thing was that my dad never had any issue with me staying there. He never said it was too much, even though I was there probably three weekends out of every month. It was my safe haven, my escape. What I didn't know then was that a lot of the abuse my siblings endured at the hands of my father happened during those weekends I was away. They told me later about coming home one time to find that shit had really hit the fan.

It's strange, isn't it? How we could live two completely different lives simultaneously? There I was, feeling safe and normal at Alice's, while back home, my siblings were weathering storms I couldn't even imagine. It's like the universe was giving me these brief respites, these glimpses of what a normal childhood could be like, even as chaos reigned at home. Alice and her family probably never knew what a lifeline they were throwing to me, how those weekends at their house were keeping me afloat in ways they couldn't possibly understand.

BENEATH THE SURFACE, I was nurturing a quiet insurrection, the seeds of which I scattered onto pages in a silent flurry of defiance. With the stealth of a cat burglar, I slipped my paper rebellion past my father's ever-watchful eyes. It soared on the wings of secrecy to my granny's haven in Alabama, each word heavy with the burden of our trials. My sister hid the card we had found from the Cat Lady, our dad's girlfriend, in our dad's briefcase, and eventually brought it back with us to Alabama and gave it to Granny who ended up using it in our custody hearing.

Dad's rages seemed to mount to a more violent degree. He demanded we affirm his version of the truth surrounding my mother's indiscretions and arrest, a truth laced with bitterness and accusation. It was a perverse ritual of confession and punishment, his way of controlling the narrative.

Somehow, Dad considered himself a mind reader, convinced he could sniff out any hint of conspiracy among us. When he decided we had been in cahoots with Mom's half-baked freedom plot, he'd let loose his fury, a hailstorm of discipline that made the Old Testament God seem a tad lenient. His tirades were as endless as a Monday, leaving us to wonder if someone had broken a mirror over our collective heads, cursing us with endless years of ferocious bad luck.

In reflecting on those tumultuous days, I understand now that what felt like a breach was, in fact, a bridge crossing over from the unchecked cruelty of a father's wrath to the possibility of safety and the whisper of hope. But even with this understanding, the memory of that revelation and the stark nakedness of our plight in the fluorescent glow of that bowling alley remains etched within me as a reminder of the power of secrets and the cost of their keeping.

ON THE SURFACE, we were siblings bound by the usual ties. But beneath lay a chasm carved and deepened by our father's hand. He had a knack, a cruel sort of genius, for pitting us against one another as though family were a competition no one truly wanted to win.

"Why can't you be like Ginny?" he'd goad, his voice a

sharpened edge aimed at the tender heart of my brother's confidence.

The scenes play back like a film in slow motion: my brother, lost in the labyrinth of algebra, with every wrong answer another slice into his self-worth. And then, my father's voice, a crescendo of contempt, branding him with the label of "stupid" until it became a confession ripped from his lips. It was a game for my father. I was always brought in as the unwitting closer, delivering the correct answer as though it were the final blow, not of triumph, but of betrayal. The snap of his head, the boastful leer as he compared us, was his way of teaching, if you could call it that.

Mary bore the brunt of childhood's unkindness with a courage that went unnoticed, stood at barely five-feet-four, and carried more weight than a child should bear, both physically and emotionally. At school, she was the canvas upon which crueler kids painted their jeers. The epithets of childish malice, "Booger Lady" and "Chubby Chicken," cut to the bone.

But at home, after Mom's arrest became a permanent shadow in our lives, Mary assumed the mantle of matriarch prematurely. The kitchen became her domain, the meals her responsibility; every dish washed was a testament to a sacrifice no child should know. She set the alarms, readied the bathwater for my father, and became the metronome to the rhythm of our father's demands. This young girl, still caught in the throes of seventh grade, shouldered burdens heavy enough to bend the strongest of wills.

Mary was the unspoken pillar upon which we all leaned, her strength a quiet constant that held us together even as the ground shifted treacherously beneath our feet. Her resilience was not the kind celebrated in stories of heroism; it was the silent and enduring type that keeps the world spinning when all else falls apart. She was more than a sibling; she was the unsung hero who mothered us in the darkest of times.

I came to feel that my siblings were angry with me and with the benefit of hindsight understandably so. As I later learned from them, I missed a lot of the beatings they endured when I would spend the night at Alice's house, and their resentment built. When I was at home, it seemed like Mary and I were always embroiled in some kind of battle, undoubtedly as a result of this tension.

We really didn't know anything else. We had been through so much trauma together and never saw anyone model a productive, affectionate, loving relationship, or even one where someone could express their feelings safely without risk of reprisal.

OVER THE NEXT YEAR IN GERMANY, my sightings of Mom were scarce and fleeting—behind bars, in a courtroom, and once in the stark visiting room of the prison. I remember Dad, in his formal military uniform, evading the truth of his abuse in court as easily as he dodged responsibility at home. The German justice system didn't press for absolute proof; a mere suggestion of guilt sufficed. The stoic words of the judge as he handed down her sentence were muffled through the tears of my mother weeping as her hands covered her face.

Mom's sentence was tempered only slightly by the

acknowledgment of her battered past, as a child. And so, she was led away to serve her time, leaving us to navigate a world without her.

Two visits to Mom in jail stand out with stark clarity. The first was a blur of confusion and fear, but the second—that's the one etched into my soul. It was after her sentencing, a final goodbye before they whisked her away to serve her time. I remember standing there, a lanky sixth grader, watching my father hand over one of my dresses for my mother to wear in court. The image of her, once larger than life, now diminished to fit into her daughter's clothes, is a cruel snapshot of that day. She was all angles and sharp edges, her tall frame whittled down by stress and confinement.

There is an indescribable heartbreak in knowing your parent will be led away in handcuffs. At twelve years old, I stood there, trying to memorize every line of her face, every strand of her hair, knowing it would be a long time before I saw her again. The guards waited until we left before they secured her wrists in metal handcuffs. The visual of her being led away with metal tightened around her wrists echoes in my nightmares sometimes.

Our next reunion was in a women's facility in Germany. The visiting room was a study in contradiction—families trying to reconnect across tables, all under the watchful eyes of stone-faced guards. We sat at a round table, other families nearby, all of us trying to carve out a semblance of normalcy in this sterile, unforgiving environment.

"No touching," the guard barked when Mom reached out to us. Her hand retreated, and with it, a piece of my heart. The rules were clear, but the longing for a mother's touch doesn't understand prison regulations.

Mom was different here—colder, more distant. But then again, so was everything else. The room, the guards, and the very air we breathed seemed designed to stifle any warmth or comfort. What do you say to your mother when every word is being monitored? How do you convey love when you can't even hold her hand?

Our visits were brief—twenty minutes, thirty if we were lucky. Not enough time to bridge the gap that incarceration had wedged between us, but too long to maintain the facade of normalcy. As we left each time, I'd steal a glance back at her, trying to reconcile this hollow-eyed woman with the vibrant mother of my earlier childhood.

I've often wondered about the woman my mother might have been if she'd chosen college over marriage, a career over my father. But life doesn't deal in what-ifs. Instead, it hands you the cards and challenges you to play them as best you can.

Years later, I find myself wanting to reach back through time, to tell that confused and heartbroken girl that was me that it's okay, that she'll survive this. That one day, she'll understand that every experience, no matter how painful, is a chance to learn, to grow, and to become stronger. Because that's the thing about life; it's built on the small moments, the tiny opportunities we seize or let slip away. It's about finding the strength to keep moving forward, even when the path ahead seems impossibly dark. And sometimes, it's about learning to forgive—not just others, but ourselves too.

– 3 –

REFUGE IN GRANNY'S QUILT

MONTHS PASSED IN THE LIMBO of Dad's sporadic fury until Granny wove a plan that would have us go and stay with her in Alabama. The loss of Mom felt like a profound emptiness, a void where once there had been at least the hope of her protection.

I don't think Granny had originally planned for us to be there any longer than a summer vacation. But when she mentioned to Dad that since school was about to end, and he was getting stationed in Oklahoma next anyway, she suggested that we come stay with her over the summer until he got settled there. When we got back to Alabama, Granny took one look at me and told me I was as skinny as a bird. She started calling me Ginny Wren and the nickname stuck. It was only after my dad visited my mom in prison and told her he planned to take us to Oklahoma that Granny sprang into action. Mom, fearful that she would never see us again, called Granny and frantically explained the situation. That's when Granny got a lawyer.

It turned out that she had been our steadfast lighthouse all along, and she had been bracing for battle. Her arsenal was filled with the resolve of love and the might of hired lawyers and investments pulled from the well of her limited coffers. She wasn't about to let us go back to our father without a fight.

During the custody trial, my dad said to the judge, "If the children, in court, tell me they don't want to live with me, I will quit the fight." The judge looked at Granny and said he was calling a quick break, and all three of us needed to be taken out of school and brought into court. My brother and I were too scared to speak up. It was my sister who said, "Dad, we don't want to live with you."

I will never forget the shocked look on his face.

Her declaration was a lifeline thrown into the churning waters of our fate. If not for her bravery, for her voice when ours were lost, we would have been swept back into the storm—back to a life dimmed by fear, a cycle unbroken, a fate unchanged. Her words were our salvation, a pivotal turning of the page that led us away from the darkness of our father's shadow and into the promise of a new day. I felt my heart beating so loudly, my palms sweating, my face red and hot. I was so scared to speak up. I looked down, playing with my fingers on my lap. I didn't want to look him in the eye. I actually felt sad for him at that moment. Incredible to admit, I know. I still feel guilty to this day that I was not able to summon the courage to speak the truth in front of our father.

And so, it was settled. What had been our temporary stay at Granny's in Alabama became our permanent home.

To our uneasy surprise, our father upheld the custody arrangements. He trekked the distance from his new posting in Oklahoma to our Alabama refuge, visiting us in sporadic bursts that unsettled the air around us. His presence carried the surreal quality of a scene badly stitched into reality, as if he were an actor who'd walked onto the wrong set, denying the drama that had preceded his entrance. There we were, teetering on the edge of growth, and there he was, pretending the abyss between us, the one he had dug with his own hands, didn't exist.

His arrivals were always unannounced, at least to us. He may have worked with Granny on dates to visit, which usually centered around court dates. There were only a few times we received his visits, and they were always awkward at best. We never knew what to say to him and Granny wasn't comfortable with him taking us anywhere, yet she believed it was important for us to see him.

She was careful never to be hateful to him no matter what because she knew he would just take it out on us kids. These visits were intrusions that turned the comforting walls of Granny's house into a stage where unwanted plays unfolded. There, in her domain, he was a guest who had overstayed his welcome before even arriving. There was no debate, no negotiation. Her word was law, and her living room was a courtroom where the judge had already ruled.

Amidst this, my life's plot twisted through the awkward chapters of seventh grade. The school halls were a gauntlet, homework an unending siege, bullies the dragons of modern-day lore, and puberty a minotaur in the maze of adolescence.

In the middle of all the chaos, my body went rogue with puberty, timing its upheaval with the precision of a poorly scripted sitcom. I got my period and at five months the bleeding wasn't stopping. Granny immediately took me to the doctor where we discovered that I was severely anemic. To get the bleeding to stop, the doctor prescribed birth control pills.

After arriving home from the doctor's appointment, the security of Granny's sanctuary was pierced by a surprise visit from my father—an unwelcome echo of a life we were trying to forget. His interrogation cut through the silence.

"What's in the bag?" he asked. A simple question elsewhere, here it was a grenade with the pin pulled.

"Oh, nothing," I said. He beckoned for me to come and sit on his lap.

So, there I was, a teenage girl with a bag of birth control pills I didn't want my explosive father to find out about, sitting on his lap like an oversized child. The absurdity of it was palpable, even to my young mind at the time. I think I mumbled something and then ran off to my room. Granny explained the situation to him later.

Those two years nesting in Granny's care were a fortress built in the chaos, and a steadiness I had never known. The rumblings of my father's past actions became a distant thunder; my own storms were acknowledged and tended to, and I learned that stability wasn't just a fairy tale, but something you could wrap around you like a warm and secure blanket.

Granny's home was a modest 1960s ranch house, nothing fancy, but it was our sanctuary. The living room walls were adorned with wood paneling, a popular choice back then, and the kitchen and dining room flowed together, united by a sea of green linoleum flooring.

In the sweltering Alabama heat, Granny's electric skillet was her secret weapon. She'd plug it in instead of firing up the stove, a small act of rebellion against the oppressive Southern summers. We only had one window unit for air conditioning, a luxury Granny would switch off at night to save money. On particularly stifling nights, I'd abandon my bed for the relative coolness of the living room couch, chasing the lingering chill of the day's air conditioning.

Food was simple, often scarce, but never absent. My aunt recently reminded me of the times we'd open cupboards, hope dwindling with each bare shelf, only to watch in awe as Granny conjured meals from seemingly nothing. Hot dogs were a staple, as were chicken and rice. Sometimes, Granny's coworkers from the factory would share their farm bounty: bags of green beans, juicy watermelons, and fragrant cantaloupes. Those were feast days.

The child support from my dad was meager, a measly $500 for three kids. But Granny, with her factory job and her magic touch in the kitchen, made sure we never felt the sting of want. She gave us all we needed, even if it wasn't always what we desired.

Space was tight in that three-bedroom home. My brother, the lone boy, got his own room while the rest of us girls played musical beds. Aunt Kathy and my sister Mary shared one room while Granny and I occupied the other. I remember longing to be with the other girls, but there was comfort in sharing a bed with Granny, her presence a balm for the traumas we'd endured.

Looking back, I can see how hard it must have been for Aunt Kathy. One day she's an only child, the next she's sharing her home with three traumatized kids. And there I was, the sickly one, anemic from months of nonstop periods, naturally drawing more of Granny's attention. I felt it created a tension, a subtle favoritism that didn't go unnoticed.

Granny split from my grandfather after a three-part saga that finally reached its end, and found herself cradling the fragile world of three children shadowed by abuse. At fifty-something, her life's script was rewritten. She was a single mother to the young souls scarred by life's harsh beginnings in the second act of her life. She was also still raising Kathy, who is only six years older than me.

Granny, with the endurance of a saint and the grit of a soldier, faced poverty with a stubborn chin. She was a testament to the women born of harder times and still harder resolve. Her days started before dawn, rising at four thirty to make it to the factory on time. We'd wake to an empty house, left to our own devices to catch the school bus. The dynamics between us kids were complicated. My sister and I were like oil and water, our fights epic battles of hair-pulling and scratching.

When we'd return home from school, the house would still be empty, holding its breath until Granny returned. She'd arrive, sinking into her chair with a glass of ice water, allowing herself a moment of rest before changing and starting dinner.

In that small house, with its green linoleum and window unit, we were building a new kind of family. It wasn't perfect,

it wasn't always easy, but it was ours. And at the center of
it all was Granny, working miracles with an electric skillet
and a heart big enough to take in three broken children and
make them whole again.

The foundry where she worked, a sweltering inferno
of metal and fire, became her battlefield. There, amidst the
screech of grinding machines, she toiled to smooth the
tracks of tanks, her hands steady as she carved order from
the steel chaos. She would stand there all day, grinding them
down until they were smooth enough to be part of a tank's
rolling tracks. It was brutal, unforgiving work. Each day,
she emerged from that industrial Dante's *Inferno* with her
clothes clinging to her like a shroud and the distinct scent
of scorched metal seared into her skin—a perfume of pure
labor. She wore black steel-toe boots, and she came home
with her hair still tied up in a bandana that was used to
protect it from the sparks as she worked at grinding all day.

Granny would come home after standing on her feet all
day, every part of her body screaming in protest. Her fingers
ached from gripping the grinder; her back protested from
hours of bending over metal. All she ever asked for was ice
water to be put in the freezer fifteen minutes before she
arrived home. It meant the world to her.

In Granny's kitchen, under the harsh buzz of the
fluorescent yellow lights, I was her apprentice. I stood by
her, learning the sacred biscuit recipe passed down like a
family heirloom. It was more than cooking; it was an act
of communion. This shared ritual had roots reaching back
to her childhood days when she stood beside her own
grandmother and a whole lineage of women wielding rolling

pins like scepters. Helping her cook every night became my thing. Maybe it was because I saw how tired she was when she'd drag herself home from that foundry.

I wish I could've done more, but at least I had my chores. In the summers, Granny would leave us a list each morning before heading off to work. Mine always included sweeping the back porch, which was no small feat with the forest right behind us and squirrels treating our porch like their personal playground. I'd sweep and then leave out a peanut butter toast for those furry freeloaders—Granny's orders. Then it was mopping the kitchen floor and doing a load of laundry.

After dinner, it was dish duty for us kids. No fancy dishwasher in Granny's house, just good old-fashioned elbow grease. We'd pair off, my sister and I versus Kathy and my brother Mark. One team washed, the other dried and put away. We'd alternate nights, grumbling all the while but knowing better than to argue.

Kathy, being older, often escaped to her boyfriend Gary's house. Lord, did we give that poor boy hell! We'd spot him talking to some girl at school and run straight to Kathy with our report. Gary would plead with her, "Can't you control your nieces? They're violating my privacy!" We'd holler, "Hi, Uncle Gary!" in the halls just to watch him cringe. But wouldn't you know it, they're married to this day!

I went through my rebellious phase, of course, and started smoking cigarettes for a bit. Granny tried to spank me for it, bless her heart. I nearly laughed as her gentle swats were nothing compared to what I'd been through before. I almost wanted to give her pointers, but I bit my tongue. My rebellion was pretty tame, really. Good grades, no drugs. Just a smart mouth and a stubborn streak a mile wide.

Granny, though, saw right through my tough act. "You're so beautiful," she'd tell me. "Keep those grades up." She was my cheerleader, my rock. Sometimes she'd invite me shopping, just the two of us. "You can get one outfit," she'd say, and I'd feel like the most special girl in the world. It wasn't much—a shirt here, a pair of pants there—but it meant everything.

I threw myself into school activities—flag twirler, flute player in the marching band— and Granny made sure I had what I needed, even renting that flute for me. When I made the dance team my freshman year, I was over the moon.

During the summers, as soon as Granny was out the door to work, we'd park ourselves in front of the TV for a soap opera marathon. On good days, we'd drag ourselves outside to work on our suntans. Being military brats had its perks; we could use our ID cards to get onto Fort McClellan and use their pool. We'd sign Kathy in and spend the whole day there, feeling like we were living large.

We'd slather ourselves in Johnson's baby oil mixed with iodine, thinking we were so clever. Absolutely no sun protection, of course. But wait, it gets better. We'd hold up sheets of tin foil to our faces to maximize sun exposure. I swear, it's a miracle we didn't fry ourselves to a crisp.

Every week, we each got our own two-liter bottle of soda. It was our little luxury. I always thought mine was Mellow Yellow, but Kathy swears it was Coke. We'd mark the bottle with a pen to keep track of how much we'd drunk. Little did I know, my brother Mark was playing us all. He'd erase my line, draw a new one, and help himself to my soda on top of his own. Sneaky little devil.

Privacy was a foreign concept in that house. With five people and only one and a half bathrooms, you learned to be quick. The full bath with the shower was prime real estate. I started getting up at the crack of dawn just to ensure I could shower before school without someone pounding on the door.

It's funny how these little details stick with you. The soda battles, the sunburns, the shower scrambles—they were all part of the tapestry of our life with Granny. It wasn't perfect, but it was ours. We were a bunch of mismatched pieces trying to fit into a family puzzle, and somehow, under Granny's watchful eye, we made it work. Those summers, with their soap operas and squirrel feeding and sneaky soda drinking, were a kind of chaotic paradise. I felt it was a time of healing, of learning to be kids again after everything we'd been through. And at the center of it all was Granny, working her fingers to the bone to keep us fed, clothed, and loved. I didn't realize it then, but she was teaching us about making a home out of whatever life hands you. Those lessons have stuck with me far longer than any sunburn.

Money was tight in Granny's house, practically non-existent, and worry was always etched onto her face. A memory emerges that makes me cringe with guilt to this day: New Kids on the Block was all the rage back then, and they had a phone line where you could call and hear messages from the band for $1.99 a minute. In my infinite pre-teen wisdom, I figured if I called and hung up before the minute was up, we wouldn't get charged. So, I kept calling, over and over, hanging up each time before the minute was up.

Well, the phone bill came, and it was $800! I can still see Granny's face, the worry lines deepening as she tried not to cry. Of course, none of us fessed up. She called the phone company, desperately trying to work out a payment plan. The poor woman was in tears, literally crying on the phone because she didn't know how she was going to pay for it.

To this day, she doesn't know it was me. The guilt eats at me sometimes. I look back now, and I'm mortified. Maybe she'll find out if she reads this book, or maybe I'll anonymously send her $800 one day and call it even. But God, the memory of her crying on that phone . . . it's a stark reminder of just how tight things were.

And it wasn't just day-to-day expenses she was juggling. She was still carrying the debt from when my dad had asked her to max out her credit cards for my mom's legal defense. He never paid Granny back for that, the bastard.

I realize how much Granny gave us in that little house. It wasn't just a roof over our heads or food in our bellies. It was stability, love, and the chance to just be kids again. She worked her fingers to the bone in that sweltering foundry, came home dog-tired every day, but still found the energy to nurture us, to see the potential in us that we couldn't see ourselves. In her own quiet way, she was teaching us about resilience, about making something from nothing, about the power of unconditional love. Those lessons, more than anything else, are what I carried with me when we left, and what I still hold onto today.

Years trickled past like the sweat down Granny's brow in the foundry until retirement came in her mid-sixties. Yet stillness was never hers to claim. Her nights were spent as a receptionist who greeted the twilight hours with a vigilance that lasted until she was eighty-six and the nocturnal sentinel of an assisted living community. Her life, a mosaic of unending nights and days spent in the care of others, stands as a testament to the endurance of a woman who bore the weight of generations and, in doing so, taught us the meaning of strength and the dignity of work.

But you know, sometimes life throws you a curveball in the best way. One day, when I was in 8th grade, Granny got a call from an old friend of hers named Vern. She had worked with him back in Michigan when she was a young woman and raising her youngest kids. He was the superintendent of the school district she'd worked for. His wife had passed away about a year before, and he wanted to know if Granny would go on a date with him.

Well, she said yes. This man drove all the way from Michigan to Alabama to see her. They hit it off right away, married shortly after, and you know what? He paid off all of Granny's debt. Just like that, the weight she'd been carrying for years was lifted.

It was like watching Cinderella in real life, except instead of a glass slipper, Prince Charming came with a checkbook and a heart big enough to love a woman and her motley crew of grandkids. After years of struggle and sacrifice, Granny finally caught a break. And let me tell you, if anyone deserved a happily ever after, it was her.

- 4 -

MOM'S DARK WAR

IT SEEMED LIKE WE HAD JUST GOTTEN USED TO our new semblance of stability at Granny's house, with its predictable rhythms of school, chores, and homework, when, like the plot twist you never saw coming, Granny received the call that my mom was getting out of prison on early release. I remember the mix of emotions that washed over me when I heard the news—relief that she would be free, but also apprehension about what her return would mean for our family. A few weeks later, she was on a flight headed to Alabama.

We picked her up from the airport, and I was struck by how cold and emotionally turned off she seemed to me. It was like the years behind bars had hardened her, creating an impenetrable wall around her heart. I wanted so badly to reach out to her, to feel a connection with the mother I had missed for so long, but she remained distant and aloof.

Getting used to Mom again was like welcoming a

stranger into our home. Prison had changed her in ways I'm still trying to understand. She spoke of Adele, a German woman she met in prison, convicted of her involvement in several murders and kidnappings. She had become Mom's confidante behind bars. Mom kept a box of Adele's things, a tangible link to a world we could never fully comprehend.

About two months after her return, my dad called to say hello. I picked up the phone, not expecting anything out of the ordinary. "Mom is home now," I said, almost as an afterthought. There was a pause at the other end of the line, a moment of hesitation before he asked to speak with her. I remember the conversation being brief, just a few short exchanges before they hung up.

Little did I know that this seemingly insignificant phone call would be the spark that reignited their relationship. Before we knew it, we were leaving for Oklahoma, and I had to say goodbye to my dreams of high school stardom. Looking back, I can see how this phone call set the stage for everything that followed—the turbulent years of their on-again, off-again partnership, and ultimately, the impact it would have on me and my siblings. It's strange to think that such a small interaction could have such far-reaching consequences. But that's the thing about life—it's often the little moments, the chance encounters and fleeting conversations, that end up shaping our destinies in ways we never could have imagined. As I navigated the ups and downs of my parents' tumultuous relationship, I would come to learn that lesson time and time again.

Before long, there was a revival of the union nobody wanted. My mother didn't even tell my granny we were moving, so we left without telling her. The U-Haul stood like a monument to futility, swallowing the remnants of our brief respite. Every box loaded was a testament to the great unmaking Granny had fought so fiercely against. Her savings and sacrifice, lawyers and courtrooms, were now rendered moot.

As we were uprooted to Oklahoma, it was not just our physical belongings that were packed away but also fragments of the fragile peace we had crafted in Alabama. And there, in the center of the relics of our childhoods, boxed and sealed, I felt that we carried unseen scars and imprints of a past that clung to us as tightly as the shadows that stretched long into the twilight of our family's history.

Mary, barely at the cusp of adulthood, carried the weight of change at seventeen when she was going into her senior year in high school. Mark was just starting college. From my observations of him, I felt his journey was tangled in its own bramble of hurt. In the shadow of our father's tyranny, it seemed to me he bore the scars from the belt's buckle, not just on his skin, but deeper, in places that don't show.

Mark was like a leaf swept up in the gale only to fall again into familiar soil. A month or two in Oklahoma was all he could stomach before he was drawn back to Alabama to a love that promised solace. The girl he went back to Alabama for and ended up marrying used to be my best friend. At eighteen, the law said he was free, but what chains of the spirit kept him bound? Our closeness unraveled like thread on an old quilt, time and pain pulling the stitches loose. The tapestry of our family was fraying, each of us a patch worn thin.

My own tale has its shadows. I remember the innocent journey from school to home in Germany that one day took a detour into darkness. A baseball field, an invitation to a dugout, a question posed by a stranger that sent my young heart hammering against my chest. I followed, my feet betraying me, carrying me closer to an edge I didn't understand. It was all a haze, but some moments stand out with sharp clarity: the suggestion of my jump rope as a tool for a game too adult for my understanding, the looming threat that was all implication and no touch.

"I think I have to go," I whispered, every step away heavy with the gravity of what might have been. He let me walk away, a grace not given to all in such sinister circumstances.

I never did confide in my mother. That day's terror became another silent stone in my pocket, heavy with the weight of unspoken things. My father's own hands touched on similar boundaries but never necessarily crossed. He found engaging in behavior like snapping my bra or giving me a wedgie comical and funny in a joking kind of way, if that's even possible. I arrived home to a scolding for my tardiness and sat down to the evening meal, each bite a lump in my throat, the unsaid filling the space between words.

In that chapter of our family saga, where peace seemed to have settled like a rare bird on our threshold, fate, as it so often does, turned the page. We were only in Oklahoma for a few months, living together and trying to make it work as a family, before Dad got sent off to serve in Saudi Arabia in the first Gulf War. I helped him pack, reading off the list of things he needed as he piled each item into his military bags. He wasn't there long before he took up with a fellow female soldier, Sophia, who eventually became my stepmother. The starkness of his betrayal of our family by physically and emotionally leaving us after uprooting us to Oklahoma was as biting as the desert winds.

The foundation we thought rebuilt was, in truth, a castle made of sand and my mother found herself sinking. I used to come home from school, and she would still be in bed. Her nadir came then, lower than the prison cell floors she'd walked. Her education had stopped where life's cruel lessons began and now it seemed to me that she lay anchored by the weight of a depression so heavy it seemed to press the daylight out of the room. The curtains would always stay drawn in her room. It was a place where the only growth was the kind that sprouted in the cracks of the sidewalk, the kind nourished by darkness.

When Dad came back from the war, we were forced to move into a depressing little house in the slummy part of town. He married Sophia, now newly pregnant, shortly after he got home from his tour and they moved to a nicer area in Lawton.

After we were living on our own, somehow my mom eventually found the strength to get out of bed each day, put on a waitress uniform, go to work at a local greasy spoon, and serve up meals with a smile that cost her more than the patrons could ever tip. Our lives were a landscape of hardship, our home a waypoint for the lost, and the overgrown yard a marketplace for the currency of despair.

Dad now lived a life apart from us. His new family sprouted and took root quickly. He adopted Sophia's children and so we gained two stepsisters and a half-brother from his endeavors, new branches grafted onto our fractured family tree, growing in directions we never anticipated. Mary spent a lot of time at my dad's home with his new family. Our stepmom and my sister had babies within two weeks of each other. So, Mary benefited from some extra help when she spent time with them. As for me, I didn't feel comfortable there and stayed away as much as I could.

In youth, my heart was a closed door to them; the kinship was marred by our father's dark legacy, his hands dispensing a litany of abuses as routine as the dawn. I felt like his sickness polluted the air we breathed. I hold a stark memory, crisp as a snapshot: my youngest stepsister, only five at the time and small, lofted high and then flung onto the bed by my dad as if she were nothing more than an object, a thing devoid of pulse and breath. I watched, a sentinel too young for such horrors, thinking, "This is twisted. This is not the shape of love." My stepmother withstood this for a relentless span of seventeen years before she, too, sought an exit from the madness.

My stepsister Joy and I have gone from emotional light-years to just an hour down the road from each other, proof that time does indeed shrink space. We've inched along the tightrope of our shared history, crafting a kinship that's as sturdy as it is surprising, given the shambles we started from.

In the aftermath of my father's abandonment, my mother's heart found another beat to follow. As she found romance, I felt her role as our mother wilted. She receded from our daily lives and became a specter that haunted the threshold every few weeks. Her presence was no more than a roll call for the living. It seemed to me she always prioritized her romances over us kids. She'd go for two or more weeks without coming home to check on us. We had no car, no money. We used my sister's food stamps and walked to the grocery store to buy food.

There I was, teetering on the edge of adolescence while my sister stood on the newfound precipice of motherhood. The mantle of caretaker fell on our unready shoulders once again. We learned the currency of survival: how to stretch a food stamp into a meal, and the number of bags we could bear on the journey from store to home. Our kitchen was a battleground where we fought hunger with the blunt weapons of a hot plate and a pot. It was a silent war, one of endurance, waged in the quiet corners of a life where parents existed in echoes rather than actions.

The resilience we honed was forged from necessity, from knowing that if we did not care for each other, no one else would. It was hard, yes, but within that hardship lay the unspoken understanding that we were our own keepers, our own uncertain salvation.

CRADLES AND CRIBS

IN THE TURBULENT DAYS of self-reliance, I stumbled upon a boy named Noah—a young man, really. Dressed in military garb, he was older and seasoned in ways I couldn't quite fathom. There was an edge to it, this relationship, with its uncomfortable arithmetic. My sixteen to his near twenty-one. Yet, in the throes of our shared survival, he became an anchor that ensured my sister and I kept course through the storm of our days, an approximation of normalcy in the ritual of school and college.

Noah lived in the barracks on post, but basically moved in with us. My mom spent all her time with her boyfriend and would only come home once or twice every two weeks to check on us; then she would go back to her boyfriend. So, there I was in tenth grade; my sister was super pregnant, and my mom was nowhere to be found. Noah was four and a half years older than me, and he looked out for Mary and me and made sure I got to school and she got to college because, of course, we had no transportation.

Noah became the semblance of family at a time when the concept had frayed at the edges. There was care in his actions, a guardianship that filled the empty spaces our parents had left behind. But, as the wheel of time spun, 10th grade soon turned into 11th, then 12th grade, with almost no parental supervision. Noah was my only anchor in a world that felt upside down. By junior year, I too had become pregnant.

I posed for my senior pictures, my belly swollen with nine months of pregnancy. Most girls were worried about their hair or their smile; I was calculating how to hide a human being growing inside me.

"Just from here up," I told the photographer, gesturing at my chest. But something in me rebelled at the last moment. "Actually, no. Let's do the full preggo shot." Why not embrace this version of myself? God knows, I'd spent enough time trying to shrink, to disappear.

A few weeks later, I was staring down the barrel of a phone call I never thought I'd have to make. Picking up the phone to dial my dad, who'd become more like a stranger over the past half year, was like swallowing pride the size of boulders.

"Hey, Dad, it's me. I need to pay for my senior pictures." That conversation echoes in my head because no kid should ever have to beg for something as trivial, yet as monumental, as senior photos.

Noah and I were married by then, playing house in a shoebox apartment that smelled perpetually of ramen noodles and desperation. I finished out the summer in a haze of morning sickness and prenatal vitamins, then faced the gauntlet of public school. Those first two weeks back were a special kind of hell. Every step down those linoleum hallways felt like a walk of shame as my classmates' eyes burned holes in my rounded silhouette. Their whispers followed me like a toxic cloud.

Salvation came in the form of an individualized education program. Oklahoma, in a rare burst of progressivism, had established a school for pregnant girls. It was a harbor, staffed by public school teachers but housed in a separate building near the hospital. Half-days, no judging eyes, just a bunch of us girls united by our swollen ankles and shared terror of impending motherhood.

I delivered my daughter, Kate, and got a whopping two weeks off before being thrust back into algebra and American literature. But now, everything had shifted. I wasn't just a teenager anymore; I was someone's mother. The weight of that responsibility settled on me like a second skin, both suffocating and strangely comforting.

Little did I know then how the patterns of my past—the abuse, the trauma passed down like some twisted heirloom—would shape my future. But even in those early days, a seed of resilience had been planted. It would take years to bloom, but it was there, waiting for the light.

Despite the fact that Noah came from a much more stable family life than I did, he was nevertheless too young to embrace the responsibility of fatherhood and being the provider for our family. Or maybe I was too much of a free spirit, and something in him bridled at putting down roots with us. But he seemed to be self-sabotaging his chances at steady work that would have provided for us at every turn.

"No, no, we don't do that," I snapped after he had failed yet another physical training test which prevented him from putting food on the table for us. I repeated this creed born from the trenches of having to fight for every scrap of stability. You honor your word, even when the exit is in sight—that was my belief.

Then California beckoned us with the promise of a fresh start, so we picked up and moved to San Francisco where our first port of call was moving in with Noah's parents. It was there that the clarity of our differences sharpened. We were two halves of a mismatched pair, walking in parallel lines that never should have crossed. No darkness of abuse clouded our days, only the stark light of our mismatched dreams and desires. He found his calling in the sanctity of home while my spirit chafed at the idea of stillness and domesticity.

"I don't do dishes," I told his parents. Without humility or gratitude, I let myself be catered to by two people trying to do their best for their child, as I was mine. I let my anger get the better of me. I wasn't going to college like I wanted. Instead, I was working as a secretary through a temp agency. I didn't see my life working out this way.

I look back now and realize they had way more of a positive impact on me than I gave them credit for. They were my first role models in what a positive working relationship looked like between two people. Noah's dad was retired so he did housework and cooked most of the meals, while Noah's mother was still working. They supported each other, never said a bad word about each other, and communicated, you know, like how people are supposed to. But maybe there is truth in the fact that you can't recognize what is unfamiliar. I had never seen adults interacting that way with each other before, so I couldn't appreciate it at the time. As I said, hindsight is 20/20 and you could say I have reverse gratitude for not only the grace they showed me but for providing me with a new perspective.

Given Noah's seemingly healthy role models, I could never understand what seemed to be his inclination to escape his commitments to me and our new baby. Maybe he was no more ready to be in a committed relationship than I was. For my part, I was frustrated that I was wasting away, working as an office temp, miserably at the mercy of others at any time of the day. I did nothing but stand at the photocopier, printing copy after copy, or nothing at all, for days at a time.

After playing house for a while, living under his parents' roof, we both agreed that our attempt at marriage wasn't working. I was homesick for the red earth of Oklahoma and out of place in the big city where the only way up seemed to involve lots of money. We finally decided to part ways, though Noah did the right thing and drove our daughter and me back to Oklahoma.

So, there I was, twenty years old, armed with a high school diploma, a year of college, and a heart hungry for autonomy. It was in Oklahoma where I sought to reclaim myself, to build a life on the bedrock of my own making. I was ready to make my dreams come true.

– 6 –

GREASY APRONS AND TEXTBOOKS

BACK IN OKLAHOMA, I set about trying to finish my education. There was a little corner on campus at Cameron University, where I had enrolled, that was tucked away from the rush, and where numbers danced and futures were calculated—they called it the accounting lab. It was rigorous, like tackling math with a side of Greek philosophy. But before the debits and credits captured my mind, I fancied the badge and blues of law enforcement. I was certain I'd wear the uniform and walk the beat in Lawton, Oklahoma.

As I started the testing process for the local police department, I paused. There's power in asking oneself the right question at the right time. "Is this the life I'm chasing?" As fate would have it, a chance encounter with a Texan studying accounting was what tipped the scales. Her simple admission, "Yeah, it's very fucking hard," was somehow more inviting than daunting. The next morning, I shifted gears—no more criminal justice for me. I was set to be an accountant.

Soon enough, I was in class and playing the role of the stretched-too-thin student mom when the CPA instructing us, wise to my world of daycare and double shifts, offered a check-in.

"How are you doing today, sweetie?" she asked.

I confessed to the ache that was sitting deep in my bones.

"Do you want to know how to do this stuff?" she asked. Her advice was a mix of grit and tenderness. "Get out of bed and put one foot in front of the other."

That was the nudge, the proverbial boot to the backside, I needed. Life's alignment wasn't waiting in the wings; it was squarely on my shoulders. From that day on, I owned it and steered through life's tight turns with a steady hand.

I referenced the advice of my mentors, the word of God, or the lyrics of Taylor Swift when I needed a crutch, but I ultimately picked myself up by my bootstraps. I embraced the power of my narrative and calculated, balanced, and forecasted a life of my own design.

Meanwhile, I still had to pay the bills, so I was waitressing at Ryan's Family Steakhouse, a restaurant known for its bustling crowd that attracted a lot of military folks. It was just another day of the busy lunch scene there when I scanned the line for tables without kids because, let's face it, fewer crumbs meant faster turnover and more tips. As I came out of the kitchen, I noticed two men in uniform already seated in my section. I walked over, introduced myself, and asked what I could get for them. Both were friendly and easy on the eyes, but the one with the dirty blonde hair and a crooked smile caught my attention. He asked if I had a sister who worked at the local bar. I laughed and said, "Nope, my sister's got kids and stays home with them." We had a connection, but my Southern manners wouldn't let me ask a guy out.

As I tended to other customers, I saw them leave. I glanced up and there he was, leaning against the gumball machine. I shook the thought of him out of my head and went to clear their table, half expecting a phone number scribbled on a napkin. But there was nothing, just a generous tip from Mr. Blondie. I figured he liked me, but life was too hectic to dwell on it.

Being a single mom meant hustling to support my family. My days were a blur of college classes in the morning and restaurant shifts in the evening, seven days a week. I had a chip on my shoulder the size of Texas, determined that my kid wouldn't want for anything. I was going to make something of myself, and I made sure everyone knew this job was just a stepping-stone.

My best friend Bella lived in the same apartment complex. We hit it off in ninth-grade Oklahoma history class, and her upbeat personality and caring heart kept me laughing through the tough times. She loved hitting the clubs, but I was more of a homebody. One night, she convinced me to go to Scooters, our local country dance spot. On the way, we stopped by my sister Mary's to drop off my daughter Kate. I always made sure Kate woke up in her own bed, even if it meant a late-night pickup after clubbing.

We arrived at Scooters and scoped out the place, sipping our beers. Bella was the social butterfly, chatting and dancing circles around me. Country dancing was more my speed—follow the steps, let the guy lead, and you're golden. As I wandered around, I locked eyes with the guy from the restaurant, Mr. Blondie. I wondered if he remembered me. A pang of disappointment had hit me back then but seeing him here felt like a second chance.

"Hey, you're the Ryan's chick," he said.

I laughed, "Yeah, I think I waited on you. And by the way, I can tell you liked me; you left more money than your friend."

He smirked, "Or maybe my mom was a waitress, and I know how tough it can be."

Ouch. The slogan on my T-shirt—"Damn I'm Good"— and my short shorts weren't going to get me out of that one. At a loss for words, I blurted, "Check out my new tattoo," and hiked up my shorts to reveal a "Mean People Suck" smiley on my upper thigh.

I had just gotten the tattoo a few days earlier, on a little mother-daughter bonding trip to Texas. Mom chose a rose for her thigh, and after a day of lousy tips, I figured "Mean People Suck" was a fitting tribute.

"Did it hurt?" he asked.

"Well, it tugged a bit and hurt some, but afterward it felt like a high," I replied. "I get why people go for more than one."

I nodded at his beer and said, "Mind if I have a swig?" Then I chugged the whole thing and set the empty bottle down with a grin. He was smiling too.

"Wanna dance?" he asked, taking my hand and leading me to the dance floor.

Neither of us was Fred Astaire, but we managed. The upbeat song ended, replaced by a slow one, thank goodness. He pulled me closer, and we swayed to the country tune. Fueled by a few drinks, I blurted out, "I'm not normal, just so you know. And I have a kid."

He asked a few questions about my daughter, and just like that, the song ended, and the bar was closing. Bella and I had our rule: arrive together, leave together, and one of us stays sober. This time it was her turn to drive. We all walked out of the bar together.

"Where's your car?" I asked.

"Over there," he replied, pointing to a massive blue 1976 truck with gigantic tires and a french fry stuffed toy on the dashboard. "And by the way, I'm Jack."

"Nice to meet ya Jack, I'm Ginny." Not the kind of truck I pictured for a military officer driving, but okay.

"Can I call you sometime?" he asked.

I scribbled my number on a sticky note he pulled from his truck.

Jack hugged me, kissed my cheek, and we went our separate ways.

On the drive home, I wondered if I'd shared too much. I usually kept my daughter's existence under wraps until I knew a guy better. It wasn't about being embarrassed; I took motherhood seriously and didn't want just any guy meeting her. She was adjusting to a new place and her parents' separation, and I didn't want to pile on more changes.

"Mommy, Mommy!" screamed my three-year-old as

I picked her up from my sister's house. I ran to Kate and hugged her with all my might. Her big brown eyes could melt my heart no matter how exhausted I was from working two jobs and going to school full-time. She was the reason I pushed through every day, my purpose in life. I adjusted her glasses and gave her a big kiss, thinking to myself about this new potential man in my life and wondering what bright future might be in store for us.

IN MY EARLY DAYS AS A SINGLE MOM and trying to complete my education, each day whirred into the next like a whirling dervish of a blur. I was in classrooms by day, slung hash by night, and crammed in study time whenever the world quieted down. It was like juggling too many balls in the air—miss one and they all come tumbling to the ground. Kate, bless her heart, ping-ponged from my sister's place to daycare faster than I could keep up.

The money side of college was threadbare. However, Oklahoma's grants and a late-game scholarship were my lifeline and saved my senior year. I owe a debt of gratitude to the small but mighty Cameron University.

Although I was a student, I lived in the adult world. It was a one-bed shoebox in a corner of town so rough that you could score more than a sugar rush from our front lawn. The walls were paper-thin, and the neighbors . . . well, let's just say it wasn't the Ritz. But $295 for rent was nothing to sneeze at. It wasn't much, but it was ours—a little island in a sea of chaos.

I'll never forget the day I landed my internship at Halliburton Oil and Gas—talk about hitting the jackpot for a single mom who'd been hustling tables just to make ends meet. I was invited to go from slinging plates to a swivel chair in the corporate world. This opportunity was a real chance to build a future for me and my girl. I had finally caught a break.

But just when you think you've got it all mapped out, along comes a detour you never planned for. It was in this corner of life, right as I was rounding the bend on my degree, that Jack walked into the picture. Jack was that detour. Instead of chasing my independence and future, I drew towards the dream of a family and a life together. I can't say whether I was caught up in the idea of love or providing that white picket fence for my daughter that I never had. I hadn't experienced any real stability since the years of living with Granny and I craved it desperately. I thought Jack was the answer to my deep longing for a stable home.

Meanwhile, Halliburton expressed interest in bringing me on board for good, through which I could have provided us with our own homegrown stability. Yet at the same time, Jack was packing up for Fort Riley, and somehow I found myself doing the same and leaving behind everything I'd worked so hard to build. I told myself it was for love but, truth be told, it was fear dressed up as an adventure.

Kansas was no promised land. I found myself in a new kind of solitude, clawing for a job and aching for friendship, all while Jack reduced himself to a ghost overseas. I traded in my hard-won stability for the uncertain rhythm of military life and, in doing so, I lost a piece of myself. I should've stood my ground and claimed Oklahoma as our turf, but hindsight's a luxury I didn't have back then. Instead, I learned the hard way that when you uproot your life for someone else, you better be sure it's for the right reasons because the cost of it all doesn't come cheap. Who you pick as your partner can make or break you.

IT WAS WITH THIS MINDSET that I approached my relationship with Jack. He represented a chance at the life I'd always dreamed of—the kind of life that seemed so far out of reach in Granny's modest home. The military lifestyle, for all its challenges, offered a stability that I craved after years of uncertainty. So, when Jack received orders for Fort Riley, Kansas, I saw it as an opportunity to lay down my conditions. The little girl who once watched her grandmother cry over an unexpected bill was now a woman determined to secure her future. Little did I know then that the promise of security and stability I sought would come with its own set of challenges. The white picket fence dream I was chasing would turn out to be far more complicated than I ever imagined. But at that moment, standing on the precipice of a new life with Jack, all I could see was the chance to escape the financial struggles that had defined my childhood with Granny.

After three years of dating, we married on the other side of the Texas border, sidestepping Oklahoma's syphilis test and its three-day wait, before arriving in the stark plains of Kansas where I spent months in a vacuum of no support. There I was, by the age of 25, my every connection to home severed, my job, friends, family, and life left behind. Stranger still, when the judge at the courthouse declared us married, Jack refused to kiss me. He also said he didn't want anyone to know we were married until we had our big wedding. He said if I told anyone it would be worse than cheating on him. I agreed to keep the marriage a secret. I suppose those early signs of withholding affection could have been seen as harbingers of things to come. But I was ever the optimist and fiercely believed things would work out.

In addition to being adrift in this new world, I grappled with Jack's concealed sorrow when his father passed away. A single tear was the only hint of the iceberg hiding beneath his skin, but it revealed the depth of his emotional disconnect. The truth is, Jack and I were both casualties of a panorama of childhood trauma. The turbulence of our time together was nothing other than par for the course. It was all either of us knew. He had abusive chapters filled with stories of nights cocooned in the cold confines of a car, all written by his father. The ones written by his mother were of the turbulence brought on by her romantic entanglements and the violence that bled from them. Since he was a toddler, after his parents' divorce, Jack felt perpetually on trial, his worth always in question, his identity an enigma even to himself.

− 7 −

ECHO CHAMBER OF FISTS

THE YEARS ROLLED BY in a haze of dissonance, delayed dreams, and the low-fi hum of thoughts like, *Is this all there is?* The reality was that I never knew life could be any different. Plus, there was the obstacle of helping Kate cope with her stepfather whom she didn't really get along with. Plus, all the usual challenges of adolescence. There never seemed to be time to focus on myself or acknowledge how unhappy the marriage was because my mental resources were pulled in so many different directions.

The years with Kate as a teenager were a tumultuous journey, filled with challenges that, I felt, tested the limits of our family's resilience. Our home, which should have been a sanctuary, became a crucible of tension and uncertainty.

During this difficult time, Jack's ill-timed home renovation only added to the chaos. With walls and doors torn down, we lost any semblance of order, stability, and privacy—all the things Kate so desperately needed.

In a moment of desperation, I reached out to Noah, Kate's father. Despite our past, I knew she needed all the support she could get. They reconnected, and soon after, Kate expressed her desire to live with him in California. At just 14, she boarded a plane, leaving me behind with a shattered heart. It was one of the hardest days of my life.

KATE'S JOURNEY CONTINUED to be fraught with challenges, even at her father's. Eventually, she found herself in a therapeutic group home in Northern California, where she completed high school.

As she grew older, Kate's path led her further from me. One day I received a terrifying call. Kate had been seriously injured. Unable to be there physically due to my responsibilities to my younger children, I coordinated her care from afar, relying on the kindness of friends and family to look after her.

After her recovery, Kate stayed briefly with Jack's mother in Texas. But the peace was short-lived. Within a month, she disappeared again, leaving behind only echoes of what might have been.

Throughout all of this, the pain of losing my daughter— not to death, but to circumstances beyond my control—has been a constant ache. The distance between us, both physical and emotional, is a void I've struggled to fill.

From the moment Kate could hold a crayon, her artistic spirit shone through. When she was little, our home was a gallery of her creations: vibrant paintings, intricate drawings, and sculptures made from whatever materials she could get her hands on. Her creativity knew no bounds, and

I marveled at how she could transform the ordinary into something extraordinary.

On the soccer field, Kate's uniqueness was just as apparent. While other kids were laser-focused on scoring goals, Kate had a different priority. She was always the first to help up a fallen teammate or console an opponent who missed a shot. Her coach would joke that she was our team's unofficial cheerleader and medic rolled into one. Kate's empathy and kindness stood out even in the heat of competition.

When we moved away from Oklahoma, Kate found a touching way to keep her connection to our old home alive. In her notebooks, on scraps of paper, even on steamy bathroom mirrors, she'd draw a meticulous 'U' inside every 'O' she came across. It was her silent tribute to Oklahoma, a place she missed dearly. This little habit of hers always tugged at my heartstrings, reminding me of the depth of her feelings and her unique way of expressing them.

Kate's sensitivity to the world around her was both her gift and her burden. She felt everything so deeply—the joy, the pain, the beauty, and the injustice. It was as if she was tuned into a frequency the rest of us couldn't quite hear. This made her an incredible artist and a compassionate friend, but it also meant she felt the world's harshness more acutely than most.

Looking back, I can see how these traits—her creativity, her empathy, her deep connection to places and people— were early signs of the complex, beautiful person Kate would become.

Despite the heartache and challenges, I'm proud to say

that Kate is now thriving in her own way. While our paths remain separate for now, I continue to hope that one day we can reconnect and bridge the gap that life has placed between us. My love for her remains unwavering, and I hold onto the hope that our story isn't over; it's just waiting for its next chapter.

WHEN THE THREE CHILDREN I had with Jack were small, I walked on eggshells and tiptoed around him. I had my role in the home, and he had his. I knew by this time it was a marriage of convenience because I had lost any semblance of romantic feelings towards him. I was also so scared that I couldn't make it on my own. I thought that I needed Jack to survive. I had accepted my fate. My goal was to get my kids raised and then leave. I watched romantic movies and felt a huge hole in my heart. I felt gutted. I so badly wanted someone to be tender and caring towards me and I felt a void in my life. But, still, I would have stayed for my kids. However, when I had to go back to work, Jack took away the one and only reason I stayed.

By 2015, I was standing on the embankment of a decision that had been years in the making. The children had been my orbit, their needs my gravity, and for too long, though still married, I felt like a single parent. This solo act had worn grooves into my resilience, and I found myself at the end of my rope, clinging to the last strands of patience. Summoning the courage to address this imbalance was akin to gearing up for battle. Past requests had detonated explosive arguments and the scars from those encounters throbbed with a memory of their own. Yet there I stood, weary from the unending cycles of childcare and my voice carrying the weight of a hundred silent pleas. My attempts to address the imbalance gained no ground. My words, heavy with the sediment of suppressed battles, hung in the air like a challenge.

I had a flashback to the past—an echo of the dysfunction I knew so well from my childhood. It was a critical juncture: either retreat or push forward. The result was a fury made manifest, a fist through the door inches from my head, a punctuation mark to the sentence I had dared to speak. The hole in the door was a stark metaphor, a symbol of the void in my marriage where partnership should have stood.

Early on, there were signs. I would catch glimpses of the rage simmering beneath his polished surface. I remember watching as his frustration would boil over while he was out working on his Bronco. The tools flying across the yard were a physical echo of his internal turmoil.

In the scarce moments when I was brave enough to voice my troubles, I would only find myself mirrored in blame. My concerns were twisted and returned to me wrapped in a litany of my failings. Instead, I learned to swallow my words and turn inward where I became a hermit within my own heart. The bind felt inescapable. Even though Kate was living on her own by now, I had three more young lives in my charge, tethering me to the semblance of stability that this marriage offered me. It was a paradox of trying to nurture life in barren ground and I was lost in the labyrinth of trying to make it bloom. My question was answered for me as the tantrums in our home were redirected. I became the new north of his compass of outbursts within only a few years.

Every attempt at communication spiraled into the chaos of his wrath. My expressions of struggle met with his volcanic temper. Walls in our home were punched a few times and things were thrown. I felt unsafe even though he never laid a hand on me.

Before his anger management issues became a part of our grim routine, Jack spoke of feeling trapped but never knowing how to escape. Each new approach I tried was another wall. I felt that he was a bull charging toward the red flag of his frustrations until he exploded in a rage that I experienced as a form of neglect, and the kind of abuse that doesn't leave bruises on the skin but on the heart and psyche. His warm words turned cold and sharp. Comments about my appearance—my thinning hair, the weight I carried—were his verbal bullets. Even oceans away, in the dust of Iraq, where he would travel for work, his voice could reach across continents to deliver threats meant to silence my longing for connection.

Jack wielded control as if it were a weapon. He'd say things like, "Ginny, if you don't stop calling me, I'm going to extend my trip here." Or, "If you can't take care of these kids, I'll hire someone who can," as if I was merely a nanny who was currently failing at the job.

Our marriage slowly fell apart, worn down bit by bit.

FINALLY, I REACHED A POINT in my marriage where it was as if a gong had sounded—the signal for the end. I was screaming on the outside and resolving on the inside.

The echoes of that time are still felt in the unanimous distaste harbored by my friends. Continual verbal abuse wears people down like river stones, smooth and rounded from relentless pressure until all that is left is the shadow of a former self. This twenty-year siege that I felt my marriage had become was a costly campaign; victory was measured not in winning, but in getting through it to tell the tale.

When it finally became clear that divorce was on the horizon, war was waged in courtrooms and across legal documents, draining our bank accounts, time, and spirits. Jack was a storm of a man who sought to unsettle me and anyone else within his sphere. He had entered my life, surveyed me like a plot of land he might buy, and reduced my entirety to a shoebox for his dollars and the domestic tether of apron strings. Our relationship was as much about emotional ledger-keeping as about love, and this ghost of truth would haunt our shared space.

Our history was marred with loss; three miscarriages in total had come and gone like shadows that whispered what might have been. The prescribed pills from the midwives, Misoprostol to induce miscarriage when a pregnancy is no longer viable, were meant to bring closure but only brought agony instead. My cramps were an echo of life refusing to be silenced. When the pain crescendoed beyond my threshold, I asked Jack for one thing: Take me to the hospital. His refusal stung with the cold finality of neglect.

"I have a meeting. You're going to have to deal with this on your own," he said, his words abandoning me as surely as his presence had. Vanessa, my friend, my lifeline, carried me through that storm to the safety of the hospital. There, the doctors spoke of luck, but what echoed in my mind was the perilously thin line between life and loss—a line I had nearly crossed. If I had not gotten to the hospital when I did, I could have hemorrhaged.

The final unraveling of my marriage was a covert operation rooted in the need for truth. I reached out to colleagues of Jack's company, and what they shared was the last piece of my shattered resolve. I scribbled down words like sacred texts: stories of Jack's rage that had spilled over in his workplace, of company property destroyed, of a recklessness so profound it manifested in tossing alcohol from a Dubai high-rise, disdainful of the preciousness of life and property below.

Home was the stage for our familial theater, where I played the role I loved, but it had become a cage. In the swell of my pregnancy with my third child, Jack delivered the blow of his work challenges. The pressure was on me from that moment on until a few years later when I was finally able to start working at a private equity firm. I managed to eke out a few more years of being at home with the kids full-time. My backbone, once pliable, began to solidify.

I stopped retreating. The arguments escalated in volume and venom and so did my fortitude. It was a dangerous game. Each stand I took was met with a barrage of verbal onslaughts and what I felt was the looming threat of physical blows. Yet with each clash, my determination grew as the slow, fierce burn of a woman stoking the fires of her liberation grew.

Jack lived in the basement for a couple of months before getting his own place and moving out during the first wave of the COVID-19 pandemic. Even before then, he was seeking solace—or escape—through the digital hallways of his Bumble account. Swiping through profiles was his currency of connection. The irony was not lost on me when he confessed, which was only prodded by his sighting of my friend Vanessa on the app, and his conclusion that I would find out from her anyway. My heart might have stirred with hurt, but my expectations of our marriage had long since crumbled into dust.

During the throes of the pandemic's isolating grasp, Jack moved out. And yet, he would return, dutiful as a clock's hand, to play at parenting and provide only a semblance of fatherly duty. One day, he left his computer open—a modern Pandora's box. His notes laid bare a strategy, not of contrition, but of calculated self-improvement with the sole aim of tethering me closer:

"I need to lose weight so she is more attracted to me."

"I need to make Ginny feel more comfortable around me so she doesn't leave."

JACK EVENTUALLY LEFT THE SCENE as abruptly as he had entered it. His exit was like a petulant child's flight that left me to navigate the debris of our splintered peace. I knew the steps of the familiar dance all too well: the quiet aftermath, the rebuilding of normalcy, the solitary journey back to a routine that was mine and mine alone to bear.

It was a playbook of change, not for the sake of growth, but as a gambit to keep me anchored to him. These notes, his digital confessionals, were a roadmap of manipulation, each entry a stepping-stone on a path he hoped would lead back to us, back to me. A list of changes aimed at balancing the scales he'd tipped with his own hands—a list that I, in turn, would tip toward my liberation.

In the wake of my crumbled marriage, the tremors were felt far beyond the private terrain of our home. The community's backlash was a choir of discordant voices with my friends Jessica and Madison at the forefront, clamoring to piece back the fragments of a union beyond repair. They bore witness to the disintegration and the abuse that blossomed behind closed doors, yet their chorus was one of salvation, not support.

"How can we help you save your marriage?" they asked as if the fissures could be mended with good intentions alone. I had trusted that my friends would stand by me, yet they turned me away. They were more interested in us all keeping up appearances of happy families.

My church stood as an imposing figure in the midst of it all—the church where Jack was a disciple and where I had been grafted by conversion. Our children were woven into the fabric of its doctrine and their young minds were shaped by the solemnity of its teachings. When I confided the truth to the congregation and laid bare the bones of our suffering, I distinctly felt that they were reluctant to accept it.

"There must be something we can do," they insisted in a collective blinkering.

The confession booth became an arena. Father Joseph, armed with Jack's version of our story, was quick to question my truth.

"Ginny wants us divorced, and I want to keep the family intact," Jack had said, positioning himself as the martyr seeking counsel not for repentance but reinforcement. And there was Father Joseph, echoing the doubts.

"Could you be making this up because of your own traumatic childhood?" he asked. The very notion that my lived experience could be a fiction of my own creation was a wound that no prayer could sanctify.

Today, those same people who once sought to mend what was beyond salvation now come to me, not in judgment, but in search of guidance. They linger on the fringes of the Catholic community as their own domestic facades crack.

"Can you help us?" they now ask me.

Yet in this storm, there were beacons. Aunt Kathy, my mother's younger sister, and my friend Kennedy were the pillars that held me up when the weight of existence became too crushing, and the siren call of oblivion sang to me in my darkest moments. They, and they alone, were my lifelines when I danced with the idea of my demise.

As I orchestrated the end of my marriage with the same hands that had once planned our wedding, I found myself playing the same role. I was just as strong-willed when directing flower arrangements as I was steering my course out of the rubble.

Kennedy, with her vehement disdain for Jack, became more than just a friend to me. She was a confidante and a daily testament to endurance. Our conversations, once a cornerstone of my day, ebbed with the chaos of my crumbling reality but have since found their rhythm again. She was the ear that never tired, the heart that held space for my pain, and the proof that, even when love fails, friendship can endure the most merciless of storms.

In the wake of upheaval and newfound single mother-hood, I found myself craving normalcy. The kids were with me nonstop, as they didn't have any desire to spend time with their father and his new girlfriend. I took four precious days off work after the divorce was final to move into our new house. It was a brief sabbatical dedicated to nesting and grounding in the hope that it would create a semblance of stability for my children.

After a three-year siege, the divorce was finalized and nothing kept me from my independence. We packed up the bones of our past lives and soon enough, they hung on the walls of our new sanctuary, and the rooms filled with the laughter and echoes of my children. But the process wasn't without turbulence. The move unearthed my temper and frustrations that manifested in shattered possessions and the clatter of what I couldn't hold together. My son Peter, on the cusp of adolescence, hurled the blame onto my shoulders as a reminder that, despite my best efforts, the ripples of our familial storms touched us all.

After all of this, a memory surfaces from early in our relationship: A bunch of Army football players and their wives and girlfriends were hanging out at a bar. Jack got into an argument with one of them and things began to get heated. I then realized I needed to spring into action. I said goodbye, grabbed Jack's arm, and lovingly pulled him out of the bar. I felt it was my duty to keep things calm. Probably like I had always seen Granny and my mother do during violent outbursts from my grandfather and father. I recalled the cold air on my face as we left the club, Jack's anger weighing on my arm, and a realization that I was retracing the steps of my mother and my grandmother—women who knew the art of corralling wayward men.

EVERYONE KNOWS WHAT IT FEELS LIKE to be left out in the cold. You meet someone who feels safe and secure, like a warm embrace, until suddenly they let you fall from their grasp entirely and you're left shivering. Sean, my youngest son's godfather, was that sort of cold comfort. He and his wife Madison moved off to Florida when my son was just a little guy, and although Sean made a point of visiting all his other godchildren whenever he was back in town, James and I were never on that list. Calls? Not returned. Visits? Never happened. It was as if we had become completely invisible to him.

Madison and I both sang in the church choir and became fast friends before she introduced me to Sean. They were the kind of folks you just warm to straight away. Sean was a particularly standout guy. He had his head screwed on right, more so than I did despite being older than him, and he knew how to turn a dime into a dollar in the real estate game. Sean had the all-American dream figured out, down to a science, it seemed.

When he offered to mentor me, you can imagine that I was all ears. It isn't often that a single mom gets that sort of shot so I clung to his every word. I met with him during the divorce, and I really thought he could be a good mentor. We met once and I'll never forget him saying that "relationships are the sweet spot." His secret to success was talking to the manager of a restaurant and booking the whole day at a quiet table on Fridays. Sean scheduled meetings with anyone and everyone, all day long. His enthusiasm was infectious, and he made you feel as if you could take on the world. When he upped sticks to Florida, he left behind more than just our town; he deserted his role as James's godfather and my mentor. His deception stung more than I let on.

When word got around about my divorce, Sean showed up at my place, ready to play the support card. However, he changed his course when he caught onto the fact that I was dead set on splitting up for good. Sean tried to tell me that divorce simply wasn't on the table and that I had to stick it out no matter what. Here's the thing: It wasn't as if Sean and Madison didn't know what was going on behind the scenes of my marriage. They knew that the mess I was in with Jack was more than just regular marital spats.

We all used to go on trips together, you see. One year, a whole gang of us—me, Jack, Sean, Madison, Jessica, and Nate—made our way to the Outer Banks. Halfway through the week, I decided to confide in Jessica. She was one of my closest buds back then, and I asked her straight up about the time she saw Jack losing his cool at my son's birthday party. I needed someone on my side, and I was confident that she would be in my corner of the ring. This was right after the separation, and after she sent me biblical texts and quotes about strength and marriage. After I confided in Jessica, she admitted that they saw some "things," but God could change them if I was open to change. Nice to know it was squarely on my shoulders in her eyes.

"Ginny, yeah, we've seen stuff, but Jack is trying, you know?" Jessica said instead, giving me a half-smile. "He's trying to get better. So, you gotta do your part and work on this marriage, sweetie." It felt like a clean slap across the face. It was as if seeing wasn't believing for them. It's like they saw the fire and felt the heat but instead of helping me out of the burning house, they just handed me a bucket of water and told me to try and keep the flames down as best I could.

LIGHTNING STRIKES OF CLARITY

BACK THEN, during the separation, I was with the kids more often than not and practically running the whole show on my own. When COVID hit our house like a freight train, it was chaos. It was my job to run the household hospital of fever-ridden and coughing kids. Of course, their father decided that this was the perfect time to cut communication. Jack blocked me as if I was some spam call trying to sell him fake insurance and not the mother of his children fighting a pandemic behind closed doors. So, I did the only thing I could think to do. I reached out, not just to friends, but to the community and anyone who would listen to a desperate mother's pleas.

To my surprise and absolute relief, people showed up. Strangers from my faith community stepped up where I thought friends would and left casseroles and soups right on my doorstep, like manna from heaven or something out of a feel-good movie. I was thankful; don't get me wrong, but it also stung something fierce. Here were strangers dropping off food for my quarantined little family, while the ones I'd have bet money on to be there for us were nowhere to be seen. It's funny the way you can be surrounded by so much kindness and still feel the cold shoulder of abandonment from those you count on. It was a lesson, alright—one I wouldn't soon forget. I'm grateful for the support we received, and it renewed my faith in humanity.

Here's the straight talk: Friends, family, or whoever don't have to get behind every choice I make. That's fine. But, to turn your back on someone when they're taking the hardest steps they've ever had to? That's a whole other level. It's not just walking away; it's leaving someone alone in the trenches. That's a weight that'll bear down on you, one way or another.

Cracking the icy veneer of Nate and Jessica's newly found indifference became my unexpected mission at every community function. I navigated the room with a plastered-on smile, only to be met with their aversion—no eye contact, nor a nod in my direction. It was like we were strangers, not friends who once shared secrets over coffee. I'd muster up all my courage and walk over with a "Hello" that felt more like a "Hail Mary." What I got in return was the half-hearted, polite smile and the obligatory pat on the shoulder. When I inevitably walked away, I'd chide myself with, "Why even bother?"

But then, there was the church—my sanctuary. Some folks sidled up and asked, "How can we help?" during the storm of my divorce. Their kindness was a salve, even if it couldn't quite soothe the sting of Nate and Jessica's abandonment—two friends who once shared those same pews and prayers with me.

Although the support from the church was real, it wasn't the embrace I yearned for. I couldn't help but wonder why it seemed so hard to drum up the same fervor of support for divorce as we did for births, marriages, or other sorrows. It felt like I was marked up and set aside, that I never resided in the light of newfound freedom but in the shadow of judgment. Respect and understanding were currencies I found myself begging for while battling against the tide of disappointment and the cold shoulder of a community that taught forgiveness but practiced something far less forgiving.

Since my divorce became the talk of the town, I've taken on the role of the go-to gal for women who find themselves in rocky marriages. They sidle up to me, looking for a bite of the courage they think I've got in spades.

"I'm not happy," they whisper. "What should I do?" It's an odd feeling to be seen as some kind of mentor. But if my two cents can help them find their path, then I'm all for it. I give them what advice I can and hope it gives them the power to help themselves. And yes, I won't lie—it feels good to be in a position to help. It's a mission of mine to help others in a way that is different from some of the awful experiences I have faced. Women going through these kinds of experiences need an ear to listen. They need kindness offered to them, and not to be judged as if it is their fault.

These women, they look at me and they see strength. They see someone who doesn't get knocked down easily and who holds the secret to bouncing back from anything.

But if they only knew. This resilience? I got it from Granny, truly. She was the queen of the game face, and she pushed through no matter what life threw her way. My mom had the game face too. She could get abused by my father and a few hours later be smiling at a social function with him at her side. Watching her, I learned how to stiffen my spine, square my shoulders, and march on when, on the inside, I was anything but the picture of strength they saw.

THE DAILY RIDES into the city for work with Jack always had a particular kind of silence. It was heavy and impenetrable, like a wall of quiet between us. I'd sit next to him while miles of unspoken words stretched out like the road ahead of us. It wasn't like I planned it, but looking back, that silence was the first step I had taken away from him, an early attempt at separation without even realizing it. If I talked at all, it was about the logistics of childcare or things going on with the kids. My intention to keep the conversation from veering into anything intimate, having to do with our relationship, was calculating and purposeful.

"You're distant. You're pulling away. How do we get back to us?" he'd say, looking at me out of the corner of his eye with a puzzled look on his face. It was a question loaded with desperation; a plea wrapped in the anxiety of losing control.

I had to remind myself to play it smart because every day in that car was a countdown for me and I needed to ensure that the clock ran out when I needed it to. So, I'd toss him enough of a rope, a word here or there, to make him think we were still in this together. I needed that time as I wasn't ready to jump without a net. I wasn't stringing him along for the sake of it; I was strategizing for survival, buying time until I could make a break for it without looking back.

I opened a bank account and started having my salary deposited directly in there. The moment I went back to work after eleven years off was a semblance of a plan, a way out that started to form. Ironically, Jack getting fired forced me to go back to work to support him and my family, but it also took away the only thing I ever valued: being home with my children to guide and mold them. Something I never had growing up. The marriage was done before then, but staying home with my kids was why I stayed in an unhappy marriage.

When he bought that anger management book as far back as when we were living in Oklahoma, I found myself saying, "He's trying," over and over again, like a broken record stuck on repeat. But the inevitable explosion would snap me back into the reality of his failings, only for me to be lured back in by his sweet promises and fleeting attempts at change later on. We tried couples counseling, but it was a hopeless, vicious cycle, one that I was tired of not being able to break free from.

The funny thing is, it was my hairdresser, of all people, who opened my eyes to how skewed things at home had become. There I was, sitting in the chair, pouring my heart out to someone who shouldn't have cared at all. But unlike Jack, this guy listened to me and cared about what I had to say. The idea that people wanted to hear about my thoughts and feelings without talking over or belittling me was a revelation. For twenty years, I'd been force-fed the opinions of others, as if I couldn't figure them out myself.

Jack took monthly trips to the Middle East, where he would be for about ten days at a time. During those days, I would imagine what life would be like without him permanently. In those quiet moments alone, I slowly unraveled myself from the knot Jack had tangled me into, and pictured life on my own. Could I manage the kids, get a job, and make ends meet all by myself? These questions ended up not being daydreams, but dress rehearsals for the real deal. By the time I was playing out these solo scenarios in my head, my heart was already living the reality. I was past seeking his input because I wasn't interested in fixing us anymore. I was already standing on my own and building a life where I called the shots, and my voice didn't just echo in an empty room.

I picked up the trick of mentally slipping into another life in my head as a kid. You could say it was my means of survival. During a beating by my father, I'd picture an older, taller, and tougher version of myself staring down my folks.

"I'm outta here. I'm done with all this," I'd tell them. It was my mental getaway car when the reality of abuse was too much to face. No kid should have to learn that, but I did, and it just so happened to stick. In my adult life, pulling that mental escape act wasn't a childhood trick anymore, it was a lifeline. I could close my eyes and picture a different world where my kids and I could breathe easy, laugh aloud, and live without the fear that, at any minute, the other shoe could drop.

When you're growing up in the thick of it all, you wish for that stereotypical TV family moment when a mom or a dad swoops into the room, looks you in the eye, and says, "Kid, this ain't the one for you." But that wasn't my lot. There were no parental voices of reason in my corner; it was just me trying to dodge life's curveballs as best I could. It was during these times that I wished I could have called my dad if he were still alive. One ass can spot another ass, and he saw right through Jack even when we were dating. I think my dad would have probably been a comfort to me and it would have perhaps brought us closer.

I'd daydream about a life without the yelling, the insults, and the fear—one where honesty wasn't a foreign language that none of us spoke. I swore that I would avoid the kinds of love that left bruises, not just on your skin, but on your heart too. And yet, somewhere along the way, I stumbled right back into that familiar dance of uncertainty and mistrust. Life spins a strange circle that leads you back to the start when you're hellbent on a straight shot forward. But the last thing I wanted was for my own kids to get caught up in the same riptide. I won't lie; it was daunting. Three kids are a whole lot of life to juggle alone. But I'd done it before, in my head and as a kid, and all I had to do was make it real. I had to work that visualization into something solid—a place where we were safe, loved, and, most of all, free.

By the end of my marriage, I had one clear mission: to stand on my own two feet, with my wallet and heart. And, hell, if that meant squeezing me and the kids into a tiny one-bedroom apartment, then we'd just have to cozy up and call it an adventure. As long as my children were safe and the cash in my pocket was earned from my sweat and toil, that was all that mattered. No more feeling like I owed someone for my keep, and no more biting my tongue because the roof over our head wasn't truly mine.

Looking back, I reckon there's been this pattern from the start. From my high school marriage to Noah, then later to Jack, I've gotten tangled up in romances not just for the butterflies and late-night whispers, but for the faux safety nets they spun beneath my shaky life. You name it, they offered it: financial security, a decent home, better schools for my kids. They called like sirens, and I couldn't ignore them. Even when the love ran dry and my heart was screaming to jump ship, I felt stuck because I couldn't provide myself with what they offered. They say you marry your unresolved childhood trauma, and I was no different.

When it's you and your kids against the world, the first scramble for independence starts with a solid résumé. I recruited a friend of mine and my stepsister Joy, who was skilled in rhetoric, and together we built my story, my pitch to the working world. Interviews lined up one after another for half a year but the door to opportunity seemed jammed shut. I would have taken any job to get that ball rolling, even if it meant balancing trays of food for tips or tedious secretarial work. I finally got a contractor job at The Carlyle Group through my friend Kris. However, during the height of my divorce from Jack, they ended my contract after four years. I then faced another spate of several months of hunting for work.

My kids had their share of responsibilities too. They were a part of the team, and those chores weren't just about keeping the house in order, they were life lessons in diligence and self-reliance. They knew the drill: dishes had to be put away, laundry always got folded, and rooms didn't clean themselves. Their academics and extracurriculars were to keep their minds sharp, their spirits high, and themselves out of mischief's easy reach. On the days they were with their dad, I dove into my own world of chasing deadlines, crossing off to-dos, and breathing in a bit of solitude.

The attachment I have with my children is stronger and far healthier than any drugs or alcohol. The bond I've nurtured with them is rooted in the soil and untainted by vices. The days of my son whispering, "Mommy, don't set daddy off again," are long gone. It's a connection that thrives beyond the haze of substances and the shackles of external control or negativity. It's a testament to the power we hold within to overcome, rise, and bloom from the cracks of a once unyielding surface.

— 9 —

UNEARTHING
THE WARRIOR WITHIN

THE ONLY WAY TO WORK THROUGH A PROBLEM is to walk through it. There's no magical solution, no secret escape hatch that will transport you from the depths of your pain to the life you long for. The only path forward is the one that leads directly through the heart of the storm.

When I was in the middle of life's tornados, like the one that engulfed me during my divorce and other difficult times in my life, I clung to the vision of the woman I wanted to become. I pictured her in vivid detail: her strength, her resilience, her unshakable peace. That vision became my focal point and guided me through the darkness. I recognized that woman, who might be in the distance at that moment, and saw her in vivid detail as the best version of me. I then repeatedly told myself that I needed to get over the next hurdle, and the one after, and the one after that, to become her. Visualizing my future self is everything. Without that beacon of hope, I'd be lost. It doesn't have to be a grand vision. Sometimes it's as simple as imagining myself remembering to take a vitamin or drink an extra glass of water each day.

There's no one-size-fits-all approach to surviving life's storms. Sometimes we need to lean into gratitude and positive thinking. During the low moments of life, we need to sit in silence and weed through emotions to see why we are feeling the way that we are. But no matter what tools we use, the only way to reach the other side is to keep walking, one step at a time.

Just last week, over a year after our divorce agreement was finalized, I got a text from Jack: "Why not let Peter live with me full-time? You can't seem to handle the stress that everyone else can. I got that about you. So, make the smart move. I won't reduce child support. It's ok." Sometimes the only thing to do is tell yourself that some people are as useless as buttons on a dishrag. I'm also learning to accept that I can't control anyone else or what they choose to do or say; I can only control myself and my own actions. When it comes to my ex-husband, that means going cold turkey—no contact, no engagement—as much as is humanly possible, considering we still have kids together. At the end of the day, all I can do is focus on my own healing.

When you're in the eye of the hurricane, you discover what you're really made of. You learn who and what you're dealing with, both within yourself and in the people around you. And bit by bit, you learn to let go of what you can't control and pour all your energy into becoming the person you want to be. Inner strength is about realizing that you can only control your own actions.

As I've gotten older, I've asked myself: What mark do I want to leave on this world? Whether it's being a better mother or giving people tools to handle challenging situations, what legacy do I want to create? I want my legacy to be that of a wise old lady, sitting in her rocking chair facing the sun, and knowing she did everything in her power to stop intergenerational trauma from continuing in her family.

We often marry our unfinished childhood trauma. We seek validation from partners to heal the wounds we never addressed. That's why it's crucial not to jump from one relationship to another, as I did when I was younger. I needed time to get to know myself, and I realized that I had far more childhood trauma to deal with than I initially thought. Being kind to yourself is essential, and so is recognizing that healing is a journey, not an overnight transformation.

Every challenge we face is an opportunity to practice inner peace and apply the tools we've learned. Most of what we struggle with as adults stems from unresolved childhood trauma. We're all walking around as adult children, in a sense. For me, therapy was a game-changer. There were many times when I'd go to my therapist and say, "I don't know why I'm feeling this way. I don't have the tools to work through this on my own." Like having to see my ex-husband's girlfriend at my son's games—it was bothering me so much that I was losing sleep over it. I learned that every time I saw this woman, it was a reminder that I had failed—failed my children and my marriage. But it wasn't really about her or my ex-husband. It was about me and my journey.

As mothers, we want to give our children the things we didn't have. Keeping the family intact was extremely important to me, which is probably why I stayed in the marriage as long as I did. I stayed, even though it wasn't healthy. I stayed even though I wasn't heard. I stayed through the outbursts and the huge fights. I stayed because I didn't want my kids to be the product of divorce. I stayed because I was told my religion asks that of me. I really do hope my kids know their worth and never accept less than they deserve.

Just the other night at my daughter's recital, a woman named Louise came up to me and told me that she'd been wanting to say something to me but waited until I was fully divorced. She said, "I'll never forget the first time I met Jack. My husband owns a restaurant, and I get along with everyone, but Jack rubbed me the wrong way. I wondered how you two could pair well together. And then I saw the way he grabbed your arm. I just want to let you know, I'm so glad you left."

Every time I hear a version of this story from someone else who pulls me aside with that quiet confidential tone, it confirms that I did the right thing for myself and my family, even though it's been difficult. And throughout all of this, I still have down days; there's no way around it.

If you can figure out how to manage your mental health during those low points and maybe even learn something about yourself, that's huge. Try to retrain your brain to understand that the down parts are just as normal as the highs in life. Things always turn around eventually, and your pain *will not* be a part of your everyday life forever. I relate it to a football game—you never really learn anything while you're winning. When you're winning, you know that you like to win, you taste victory, and it feels great. But you learn the most when you're down and losing. I want to be one of those wise old ladies whom teenagers love to sit down and chat with because she's open and has a lot of wisdom to offer.

It is easy to get caught up in being a victim when in fact you have been victimized by an abuser or a traumatizing situation. But we have to remember that even when it doesn't feel like it, we always have choices. What if we retrained our brains to see life as a staircase, and that each person or experience is a stair on our journey? Maybe Jack's purpose was to give me three children. Maybe his role was to show me that I don't have to take crap from people, to help me learn how to find my voice and stay true to my boundaries and what I am willing and unwilling to accept from others. Maybe he was meant to help me retrain my brain to be a better person. I don't want to look at it as what he did to me, but rather as a chapter in my life. At the end of the day, it's my life, and he played a role in it before I cut him loose and moved on. If we could just see all of these things as chapters, it would be so much easier; it's another step on the road to being kinder to ourselves.

It's like the Stoic philosophers say, there's the thing that happens to you, and then there are your feelings about the thing that happens to you. Everything is open to interpretation, to how we choose to see it. You can choose to see it as unresolved childhood trauma that becomes a vehicle for learning about yourself, growing, and moving past those kinds of people. The thing about trauma is it robs us of our natural instincts, and it then becomes hard to decipher what is normal behavior versus what is abnormal. We are then targets for people who aren't healthy for us. For me, I reached a point where it became very difficult for me to make decisions on my own; I had completely lost myself and relinquished control of my whole existence. I first became very angry with myself. But it was only when I realized my trauma affected me as an adult that I decided to give myself grace. The experience of trauma is a part of me because, at this point, it's woven into the fabric of my being. I'm not saying it's a crutch. But I do need to recognize and acknowledge it, which means understanding when I am triggered and figuring out why. If you don't know what normal and healthy looks like, it's your job as an adult to figure it out or you will keep making the same mistakes over and over again. That's what the pattern of abuse does to us.

Through all of this, I've found so much more confidence in myself—in my ability to make decisions, see things for what they are, and reach out and grab opportunities that come my way. I can look at divorce or the abuse I experienced as the death of me, choose to be a victim, or I can see it as an opportunity for a better future. If I can find my kick-ass button after my nephew's suicide, after a crazy childhood, after being a stay-at-home mom for eleven years, and then going back to work and making six figures while caring for my children, anyone can.

Jack would never have agreed to a fifty-fifty custody

split with me, so I had to spend extra money I didn't have to pay my lawyer to draft up the final agreement, which grants me custody 66 percent of the time. If I had asked for that, Jack would have fought me, but I got it. And that's a gift, a true gift because time with my children and giving them stability is more important to me than money. Winning the majority of my children's custody was a turning point in my journey. Only then could I begin the next chapter in my life—a chapter dedicated to self-care and personal growth.

I knew that if I wanted to be the best version of myself, not just for me but also for my children, I needed to prioritize my well-being. I had to learn to love myself, to set boundaries, and to surround myself with people who lift me up rather than tear me down.

In the next chapter, I'll delve into the journey of self-care that I embarked on after this pivotal moment. It wasn't always easy, and there were plenty of setbacks along the way, but each step forward brought me closer to becoming the strong, resilient, and fulfilled woman I am today. Through therapy, mindfulness, finding hobbies, and a commitment to putting myself first, I slowly began to heal the wounds of my past and build a foundation for a brighter future.

– 10 –

DIVORCE PAPERS AS LOVE LETTERS TO SELF

WHEN YOU'RE BORN INTO a legacy of fragments, where each generation before you has added to the pile of shards, you start to see the splinters in the whole picture. When you're neck-deep in a cycle of brokenness and trying to find a way out, you've got to see the cracks first. It's like you're a fish in an aquarium, swimming in circles, unaware there's a whole ocean out there; you don't know the glass walls can break. Intergenerational trauma equips each of us, with blunt objects instead of finely tuned tools, for emotional maturity. It requires a lot to begin the search to understand what right looks like and how to reach for the right tools in your toolbox of life for each scenario you encounter. Mother Teresa said, "If you want to change the world, go home and love your family." We must learn what right looks like and retrain our brains so we don't repeat the same behavior to our children.

Looking back on my childhood, I knew nothing else but my mother and father's brokenness. I remember wondering why my mother felt the need to share with us her plans to kill my father and why she had picked random men over her children. I questioned whether these things were normal but they were all I knew to be true. How do you change when you only know brokenness?

My parents were the perfect example of what not to do and their actions taught me a lot. I knew that I needed to do the opposite of everything they did but I didn't know what that looked like. But here's the thing. I did learn—mostly about what not to do, courtesy of Mom and Dad. I owe them thanks for that in a twisted sort of way. But I had to find my own way to forgive them because they came from trauma and that was all they knew. It made me determined to walk a different path, but it took some stumbling around to find what that path even looked like.

Breaking the glass wall of your aquarium is nearly impossible without a massive perspective shift. As I said earlier, it's about learning which tool is the right one in your toolkit for the job.

"Education is the one thing that no one can take from you. Make sure you get the best one you can," my dad told me once, and this advice has stuck ever since. I am grateful that despite how damaged he was, he still had some nuggets of wisdom to share with me. I carried that with me but didn't truly understand the weight of it until after he was gone. It was after his death that I learned about the shadows of his past. My father dropped out of high school while trying to escape an abusive home in Florida. At age seventeen, with more guts than plans, he hitchhiked his way up to Michigan to crash with his sister.

Life has a way of forcing decisions on us, and my dad's future was set by his sister who signed him up for the military. This was his crossroads, his chance to find some direction in the chaos he'd grown up in. Despite the turmoil, he was a bright student. He had a mind that could crack open books and soak in the words like they were sunlight. But the realities of the real world, inside and outside the classroom, granted him more burdens than any kid should be bestowed. He got his GED eventually but kept it locked up like an old attic full of cobwebs and memories too painful to dust off. My dad was ashamed and maybe that's why he hammered home the value of education to me. Maybe that was his way of making sure his scars didn't become mine.

In the opening lines of this chapter, I laid out the thorny path of generational trauma, the kind that can chain you down like a family heirloom nobody wants. I've known folks who never managed to shake it and some who don't even see it's there in the first place. Opening your eyes is step one, but you need more than realization to haul yourself out of a rut that deep. It takes tools, strategies, and a strong will to start the climb.

The fights between Jack and me could fill novels. Those blowouts left echoes in the walls—sometimes, literally, holes in the wall that Jack made—and the aftermath always played out the same: I'd snatch up my phone, step out, and spill the latest chapter of chaos to my best friend Bella or my Aunt Kathy. As I narrated the day's clash, each word was a beat in the rhythm of release, like a ritual of decompression.

But then, after the call ended and the screen went dark, the silence would settle. That's when the echoes of my own voice would start to sound like alarms. "This isn't right," I'd think as my hand rested on the curve of my belly, on nine months full of life and promise, —and that's when the weight of what I was living, what I was choosing, would really hit home. The time when Jack had coldly told a very pregnant me to vanish didn't hit full force until I heard it played back in the retelling to a friend. I spent that night in my car to sleep in peace. He never called once to see if I was okay.

As I navigated the turbulent aftermath of a relationship that felt like a storm I'd chased all my life, I found my first beacon of understanding in recognizing the echoes of my past. The way Jack and I intertwined, the dance of our discord, had the familiar rhythm of my relationship with my parents. And yet, that revelation was only the beginning of my healing journey.

Mourning the death of my marriage was akin to grieving a living person. The marriage itself was a living and breathing entity that had succumbed to an illness, its symptoms perhaps too long ignored. The loss was profound. Divorce is the death of dreams, the what-could-have-beens, and the shared ideals and hopes I once cradled for us as a family. The pain is compounded when children are part of the equation. It's not just the severing of a bond between two people, but the fracturing of the very foundation on which you've tried to build a stable life for your little ones. It's an acknowledgment that their lives will be shaped by the same brokenness you hoped to shield them from.

But even as I bore this weight, I learned to sift through the debris of my broken dreams and find among them the seeds of who I could become—someone unbound by patterns and determined to forge a new path, not just for myself but for my kids. The act of letting myself mourn and walk through the pain was not a simple task, but it paradoxically allowed me to start piecing together a new vision of family that was crafted from understanding, self-compassion, and an unyielding hope for the future.

Splitting with Jack wasn't just an end to a chapter; it felt like I was ripping pages right out of the family album. Regret and sadness swirled around me, thick as the Oklahoma dust storms. I thought that I had busted my kids' lives wide open, all because I couldn't keep tamping down my own aching unhappiness. For the longest time, I believed that if I could've scooped up all my sadness and dumped it in some dark corner, then I could've stayed with Jack and given the kids a picture-perfect family album. That thought shackled me to him for years, but the chain broke on the night of our biggest fight. The shouting match had ended and the house was quiet, but the tension hung heavy as humidity. Then came the soft patter of little feet. My oldest son, then my little gem, slipped into my room and his small voice sliced through the silence.

"Why did you set Dad off again?" he whispered.

His words hit me harder than any scream. I was flooded with fear and disbelief. How had my son come to see me as the trigger for his father's tempests? Did he think it was my job to pacify the storm? That's when the ground shifted beneath me. I couldn't let my boy grow up thinking that walking on eggshells and tiptoeing through life was normal.

I lay there in bed as my son's innocent question bounced incessantly off the walls. This wasn't just a turning point; it was a wake-up call. I couldn't be the one always diffusing and damping down. My children didn't deserve to inherit the legacy of silencing their voices to avoid disturbing the peace. That night I promised myself that there would be no more tiptoeing. It was time to boldly stride toward a life where none of us would have to shrink ourselves, even if the path I needed to take was through uncertainty.

My son's growing respect for me is like a plant that's just started to bud. It's evolving, but it hasn't fully blossomed yet. I reckon it'll take some time before he looks back and sees the full picture of how his momma stood like an oak through a storm. He still grapples with the shattered pieces of what he thought was a normal life. I suppose it will be a long while before he realizes what I shielded him from all those years. I was taught many years ago that my kids aren't going to validate me. That has to come from within. I will move mountains for my kids without them even knowing. It still pains me to see that his world, and all he ever knew in that world, was severed. One day, maybe he will realize God and the universe don't ask us to stay in relationships that aren't healthy.

But I'm not the kind of parent that folds when the going gets tough. My mom might've tossed me aside like an old rag, but I'll be damned if I ever let go of my kids that way. These children were given to me to raise, and I'm anchored in that responsibility. I come from a lineage of resilient women who might've been dented and dinged by life's cruel hands but have never broken.

Granny was a force. She was a woman who claimed me when no one else would and stood as a bulwark against a world that wasn't kind. With her do-rag and steel-toed boots, she slaved in the sweltering heat of a foundry and ground metal for hours. Yet, every day, without fail, she'd come home, fire up the skillet, and feed us with more than just food. She nourished us with love, strength, and a sense of worth. Her 'poor man's steak' and fried okra couldn't be matched by anyone.

She taught me that the heaviest load you'll ever carry is the weight of your own life. And, let me tell you, it's a burden that can make diamonds out of coal. I want to pass down her unyielding strength and tenacity to my children, not as a legacy of pain, but as a testament to our ability to rise, endure, and thrive. Granny always told me that not only was I beautiful, but even more importantly, I had a good heart and kind soul. These are things I held onto over the years. It's not the easy days that define us, but the hard ones that shape us into who we are meant to be. And by God, I'll make sure my kids see that strength in me and learn to see their own strengths.

The next hurdle I'm trying to clear is guiding my children through their own battles. When you're raised in a home where trauma is as common as breakfast, owning up to anything can feel like sticking your hand in a lion's mouth. Admit a mistake and you might just pull back a stump. Saying "I was wrong" felt like breaking an unwritten rule of survival, and I'm still breaking down my defense mechanisms in my adult life. When you come from trauma, you can have your guard up for anything that you feel invalidates you, which then has you pointing the finger at someone else instead of listening, taking ownership of your actions, and apologizing. Watch out for these moments in yourself. So, it hit me hard when my daughter hurled a memory at me like a fastball.

"You chucked our favorite Lego playset!" she accused from her car seat; her words dripped with the kind of judgment only a kid can muster. I took a deep breath, met her fiery little eyes in the rearview mirror, and owned it.

"You're right, honey, I did that," I said, the words tasting like vinegar. "I wasn't at my best and I'm truly sorry. If this is still a thorn in your side, poking you awake at night, then I'll face it with you, every day, until it's just a distant memory."

Acknowledging your fallibility to your kids is a tough pill to swallow, but that moment, raw and real as it was, taught my girl something vital about accountability and healing. I showed her that her mom could stumble, but that she could also stand up, dust off, and apologize. Because that's life, right? It's about showing your kids that you're human. You can take a punch, admit when you're down, and still get back up. It's in these moments that respect is forged, and trust is built. Children should be taught that when they mess up, you'll still be there for them. Showing them my vulnerability is the realest lesson I can give them. It's life, love, and the art of the heartfelt "I'm sorry" all in one.

When navigating life post-divorce, you quickly learn that some lessons are too precious not to pass on. Telling my kids about personal boundaries, especially when it comes to their own flesh and blood, is one of these lessons.

"We don't throw hands in this house," I tell them. "Unless it's to pull each other up, not drag each other down." I want them to understand that battles aren't won with balled fists at home; they're won with words, patience, and sometimes silence.

To anyone clawing their way out of the aftermath of generational trauma or wanting a sliver of something healthier, here's a scrap of wisdom: You already know what not to do, so you're halfway up the mountain. The only way to get to the summit is by figuring out what to do next. I found my path by lining my pockets with my own money. Earning my own keep was like finding a map in the dark. Every paycheck was a step away from my husband and a step toward freedom. I reminded myself constantly to save every dime and that soon I would get out. Money isn't just currency; it's the key to your shackles and the power to decide your direction without needing anyone's say-so. It's more than financial freedom. It's your lifeline to a new beginning.

PASSING THE TORCH

LIFE IS A JOURNEY dappled with scars and stars, and none of us walks through it without gathering a few of each. Trouble, I've learned, doesn't bother to knock; it barges right in. Some choose to bury their troubles deep, stitching silence into the linings of their lives, while others wear their scars like badges, stories inked on skin for the world to read. This book, the story of my own trek through thorn thickets and over sunlit peaks, is my testament to the alchemy of the spirit and a chronicle of how I turned agony into a force as potent as gravity.

I've watched faces lean in and eyes light up when I confess that I'm a mosaic made of broken pieces, each one a chapter from my past. This narrative isn't just mine; it's a rallying cry for anyone who's ever been sucker punched by life. I can see the gears turning and hearts yearning in those who have connected with me through their own tales of survival. They're on the brink of sharing, teetering between the comfort of privacy and the liberation of confession. The business of sharing without spilling over is a tightrope walk. There is a practiced balance of inspiring without exposing too much of the raw and tender flesh of our stories.

But that's the dance, isn't it? We find the rhythm between saying too little and too much, and maybe, in that sway, we find others moving with us and finding their balance, beat, and bravery. In the South, they call it "airing your dirty laundry." But this book isn't just about pain or dirty laundry. The muscle we gain as we hoist our burdens and forge ahead is the result of struggle. It's about transforming, not just enduring, and giving others the courage to do the same. We can't grow old without the scars of our own challenges and triumphs. Traditionally, society sought out their elders for their knowledge and strength. While we might have lost some of those traditions in Western society, aim to grow into that wise old woman or man, and be grateful for the chance to grow older and smarter.

If there's one universal truth I've come to, it's this: Stories about struggle have a way of setting a table where we can all find a seat. We rarely talk about the darker moments and the struggles that stick to us in the busyness of life, too afraid to risk them revealing our vulnerabilities. But there's likely someone wrestling with their own mind, someone drowning in silent battles, masked perfectly behind a smile.

Folks are wading through life. Some are neck-deep in murky waters of despair, others floating on an uneasy sea of pills just to get by, but everyone is lugging around their own novel of hardships. I propose that instead of trudging through our chapters alone, we link arms. There's power in lending a word, a hand, or a listening ear. Because, when the night is full of shadows, even a single candle can lead someone home. So, let's be exactly that, a beacon for each other. Freedom from judgment can go a long way to supporting someone who is struggling.

Imagine if every soul you met was part of a universal support group for life's knocks and scrapes because, let's face it, trouble comes knocking for us all at one time or another. A common thread in the fabric of life is to be dealt a hand of hardships. Why not weave those threads together to form a safety net?

Now, I'm not suggesting we all huddle in the corner and throw ourselves a sob fest. When my marriage to Jack was crumbling, my world narrowed until all I could share with friends was the need to escape the fissures and failings of what we once had. What I found out was that those people had their own mountains to climb, and it wasn't their job to haul me on their backs too. They offered a shoulder, a hand, a sympathetic ear, and that mattered. But I began to see that fixating on my woes in every conversation wasn't the balm I needed.

This was where the magic happened. My friends showed up with open hearts and sympathy in their eyes. They *listened*. Listening, my friends, is the kind of support that can move mountains. Support is about being there for the highs, the lows, and all the winding, bumpy miles in between. I realized that my friends and family could offer all the love and support they could, but ultimately, I had to be the one to walk through the fire and find the confidence and faith that on the other side would be new peace and growth. And you will know you are beginning to heal when your conversations change from talking about your woes to instead talking about and planning for your goals and your dreams. I am finally finding excitement in my future. Like a toddler taking her first steps, I get more confidence in this new skill every day.

Shortly after the divorce and the move into my own house, I felt run-down and ached all over. There I was, a hot mess, wandering the aisles of the local grocery store in a daze—the kind of dark funk that clings to your bones when life's got you in a vice. The kids were elsewhere, and I was alone with thoughts that were as gray as the overcast sky outside. Then, out of nowhere, a stranger passed by. He glanced over and paused as if struck by a thought.

"You look gorgeous today," he said to me with a genuine smile on his face, before continuing with his shopping. Just like that. He didn't want my number, or to ask me on a date. He simply wished to share a kind observation and move on.

At that moment, it was as if the universe knew exactly what I needed: a little spark of kindness, a compliment with no strings attached. How often do we silently appreciate others without ever voicing it? But that guy's simple comment cut through the fog and lifted my spirits. There's power in giving someone a piece of brightness on a shadowy day. That small gesture didn't only make my day, it became a lingering reminder of unexpected light in the dark.

From then on, once a week during Lent, my place turns into a hive of shared stories and quiet support. The gathering of souls in the safety of my living room has become a kind of ritual. There's something sacred about this circle of women who come together with their joys and burdens, ready to lay it all out with a rosary in hand. We congregate not just in prayer but in the simple communion of being together. We unwind over wine and nibbles, the kind of spread that says welcome in every bite. It's informal by design because the real communion happens in the sharing. I then guide the topics and steer the ship toward the matters of heart and spirit that too often stay locked away.

Each session starts with an intention—something or someone to anchor our thoughts and prayers. But the real cornerstone, the foundation this all rests upon, is our rule against gossip. This rule isn't just out of respect, it creates a space where trust is the currency and confidentiality the creed. If something's not ours to tell, it stays untold. Silence is as powerful as any words spoken.

This practice goes beyond faith. It has forged a community right in the heart of our neighborhood, where women know they'll be heard and held. It's a space where victories can be celebrated, and struggles can be shared. Sometimes, all it takes is knowing there's a place where your voice matters and your story will find an ear and a heart ready to receive it.

If I could sit down with you, maybe on a creaky front porch swing, as we drink sweet tea with the scent of jasmine in the air, I'd share what I've come to know about the journey from trauma to true empowerment. I'd tell you about that internal kick-ass button we all have, though some of us might call it grit, resilience, or just plain stubbornness. It's there, even if your voice has been dulled to a whisper by the weight of past hurts.

Growing up in the thick fog of generational trauma, I learned to muzzle my voice and ignore that instinctual compass within. But there comes a time when you have to sit in the quiet, listen intently, and stitch that voice back into the fabric of your being. That's what became my true north. Before I felt free from the generational trauma bonds, I felt smothered under the rubble of a one-sided conversation as my voice was lost. I'd bury the memories of conflict deep as a temporary fix to avoid the truth. It took me too long to realize that leaving was the only way to be heard.

That inner voice, once you attune to it, becomes your kick-ass button. It's an innate force that propels you forward and urges you to question and challenge. It becomes the foundation upon which you build your boundaries. Oh, how I wish I'd had boundaries in my marriage so I could have said, "Your twenty hobbies are yours, and I need space for mine."

Faith has been the lighthouse illuminating the best version of myself, even in the darkest times. It's taught me the value of unconditional love, something you should first find in yourself and in the eyes of your children and not in the arms of another.

Yes, I've dipped my toes in the dating pool recently, only to have someone tell me I was too enmeshed with my kids. As if my love for them could ever be a fault. The relationship between a mother and her children is the deepest relationship of unconditional love. And I only have one life with them, so how can I waste it? You learn, you grow, and sometimes, yes, you sever ties. Not every bridge is meant to be crossed again.

As for the community—our faith communities, our neighborhoods—we need to do more than just see the signs of struggle. We need to reach out and offer a hand, a listening ear, or practical support. My dad, a Shriner, was involved in the community but never offered, or maybe couldn't acknowledge, the help I needed. Let's be the people who do something, who say something. Let's open the doors and hold the spaces for conversation because the signs and demonstrations mean nothing without action.

If I could leave you with one last thing, it's this: Our strength is in our solidarity. We're only as resilient as the support we offer to our most vulnerable. Let's forever be the strength for those who are finding their way out of the shadows.

FINDING YOUR KICK-ASS BUTTON

As I sit here, reflecting on the journey that's brought me to this point, I'm struck by how far I've come. From the depths of abuse and trauma to the heights of self-discovery and healing, it's been one hell of a ride. But you know what? I wouldn't change a damn thing. Because every bruise, every tear, every moment of despair has led me to this place of strength and wisdom. And now, my dear reader, I want to share that hard-won knowledge with you.

First things first: Embrace the present with patience. I know it sounds like some Zen bullshit but trust me on this one. That pain you're feeling is not permanent. Given time and space, it can transform into a force that propels you forward. It's like emotional alchemy—it turns your suffering into strength.

Next up: Forge your family from those who stand firmest. Blood may be thicker than water but love and support are thicker than blood. Your tribe might be friends, relatives, coworkers, or even that kick-ass online community you stumbled upon. They're your circle of strength, your chosen family. Cherish them.

Then, set modest milestones for yourself. What does betterment look like for you? For me, it was the promise of internal peace where no one—not Jack, not my parents, not even my self-doubt—could rock my inner emotions. Find your definition of progress and work towards it, one small step at a time.

Subsequently, surround yourself with positivity, honey. And I don't mean in some woo-woo, crystals-and-incense way. I'm talking about people who lift you up, who see your worth even when you can't. My children do that for me. Find your cheerleaders and keep them close.

Consecutively, document everything. Not just for the record, but for your peace of mind. When Jack demanded my personal notes, my refusal was backed by the fortress of my privacy. Your experiences are yours alone; don't let anyone take that away from you.

Along the same lines: Journal, journal, journal. It's not just for angsty teenagers, I promise. Writing is both witness and therapy. It helps you process your thoughts and track your progress, and sometimes, it's the only way to make sense of the chaos in your head.

This one's tough but a must: Know your triggers, inside and out. If someone tells me how to drive when I'm behind the wheel, that's a trigger for me. I recognize it now, and instead of losing my shit, I might say, "I'll get us there, no worries. I gotcha." Understanding your triggers takes time and self-reflection, but it's worth it.

Hereafter, have a safe person. Someone who's okay with you calling them at three in the morning when the world feels like it's caving in. My Aunt Kathy was that person for me during my divorce. Find your Kathy. They're out there, I promise.

If you can, volunteer. It puts you in a mindset of giving, and let me tell you, it feels good. It's also a reminder that even when your own life feels like a dumpster fire, you still have something valuable to offer the world.

And lastly: Let go of history. I know it's easier said than done but holding onto all that baggage will weigh you down like chains. You can't change the past, but you can change how you view it. Forgive, not for their sake, but for your own. It's the most selfishly unselfish thing you can do.

And always remember, darling, that the death of something is always the rebirth of something else. Embrace change. Your reinvention won't happen overnight. Rome wasn't built in a day, and neither is the road to rediscovering who you are. It's a process, like a long game of football. Sometimes you'll score, sometimes you'll fumble, but the real growth happens when you're down and you have to dig deep to keep going.

So, here's to finding your kick-ass button and embracing the suck and coming out stronger on the other side! To building your tribe, setting your milestones, and slowly but surely becoming the badass you were always meant to be. The journey isn't easy, but honey, it's worth it. And remember, you've got this. Now go out there and kick some ass.

HEALING POEMS

Take My Name, Take My Life

I saw you standing at the gumball machine looking all
cute as you stared back at me. Uniform, bright smile,
and my heart swelled with intoxicating highs. Formal
balls and makeshift walls soon began to torture my
inner personality. Apron strings tied to a college degree
became my one and only dream. Reading articles
before dates became a necessity.

I took your name; you took my life.
You marched in with laughter oh so bright.
I gave heaven and you gave hell.
What about those open promises of riding broncos
into the pink sunset?
Never to come true due to the anger of life's
circumstances.

Dropped bagels on New York subways, broken vases
smashed in tight spaces put me in cages as I questioned
my role. Your love felt like alcohol in boats parted by
dusty roads caused by bloody knuckles banging on the
ocean's floor.

I took your name; you took my life.
You marched in with laughter oh so bright.
I gave heaven and you gave hell.
What about those open promises of riding broncos
into the pink sunset?
Never to come true due to the anger of life's
circumstances.

You promised me life's affections but your GPS didn't
say so. Your name was signed on dusty papers but
thankfully the judge said no. Did you mean to slice my
life with a big ole farmer's knife? I got strong and I got
tough. Those rusty telephones don't mean so much.
I got smart and I got mean, don't you see? Don't mess
with sweet, sophisticated me.

I took your name; you took my life.
You marched in with laughter oh so bright.
I gave heaven and you gave hell.
What about those open promises of riding broncos
into the pink sunset?
Never to come true due to the anger of life's
circumstances.

Stay in Your Car

Driving Fords that cost a fortune in weather that has me scorchin'. Fights during dinner made me question if we were ever winners. Seeing you pounding beers one night had me in tears. I watched your feet take flight that night as you drifted outta my sight. I was worried about your direction as I grieved and handled my own affection. Finally, at last, babe, I realized we ran outta gas while we were wearing masks. That is so fucking badass.

Stay in that car, and I promise you, life won't pass you by. Did you hear me? Did you hear what I had to say? As the years go passing by, passing by, passing by.... There, I said it and I look back. See, I was living life behind emotional bars. Must have been high on someone else's dream. Feels like tumultuous energy radiating from the deep blue sea. Follow the light, that's your beacon, and stay awake at night. Don't let another control your fate so stay and fight. No, drive that car outta Dodge and find your star. You seemed to dream it anyway. You made it so far, girl, you've made it so far.

My mind tells me to be quiet, pay attention and I will see. The latest podcasts, fancy new quads, caring about faces and spaces—all feel like an orange shirt kinda facade to me. The time you stole gives me the biggest hole. What are you hiding, baby? Everyone feels pain and I see your stain.

Stay in that car, and I promise you, life won't pass you by. Did you hear me? Did you hear what I had to say? As the years go passing by, passing by, passing by.... There, I said it and I look back. See, I was living life behind emotional bars. Must have been high on someone else's dream. Feels like tumultuous energy radiating from the deep blue sea. Follow the light, that's your beacon, and stay awake at night. Don't let another control your fate so stay and fight. No, please drive that car outta Dodge and find your star. You seemed to dream it anyway. You made it so far, girl, you've made it so far.

Beat him ... like a football team, by kindness, joy, and keeping my cute nose clean. I think about hitting. I think about punching. I think about staring him down with an ice-cold glare. But I would never. Why? 'Cause, the people who wound us don't get a say on how we clean up the blood.

Stay in that car, and I promise you, life won't pass you by. Did you hear me? Did you hear what I had to say? As the years go passing by, passing by, passing by.... There, I said it and I look back. See, I was living life behind emotional bars. Must have been high on someone else's dream. Feels like tumultuous energy radiating from the sea. Follow the light, that's your beacon, and stay awake at night. Don't let another control your fate so stay and fight. No, please drive that car outta Dodge and find your star. You seemed to dream it anyway. You made it so far, girl, you've made it so far.

"If you want to change the world,
go home and love your family"

– *Mother Teresa*

ABOUT THE AUTHOR

GIN CLIFTON set out on a mission to inspire readers to find their voices after a life of trauma and abuse. We all have a kick-ass button, we just need to dig deep, find it, and use it.

Gin is a powerhouse of resilience and inspiration, driven by a deep commitment to help others rise from adversity. As a military child, an accomplished accountant, and a dedicated entrepreneur running GinnyWren, LLC, Gin knows the importance of perseverance and grit. A single mother to four children and a lover of nature, she channels her energy into empowering teenage mothers, women in prison, and anyone seeking to overcome life's toughest challenges.

With an infectious passion for education and self-improvement, Gin's mission is to guide her readers through the process of becoming their best selves. Her down-to-earth personality and vibrant spirit allow her to connect with people from all walks of life, constantly learning and growing through these interactions.

When she is not writing or inspiring others, you can find Gin enjoying the great outdoors—whether it's hiking, kayaking, or volunteering. Based in the DC area, she juggles raising her kids with her love for adventure, always seeking to make the world a little better each day.

All yours in Kicking Ass,
Gin
www.ginnywren.com

ACKNOWLEDGEMENTS

Countless people have helped me on my journey toward helping others. I will forever offer my sincerest gratitude to each and every one of you.

To my friends and family who cheered me on and proofread my book many times over, thank you for your support and unconditional love. Kathy Nagle, whose advice and guidance always superseded any inconvenience. Vicki Clifton, whose ability to help reword and rewrite is masterful. To Nancy Schiller for all her tough motherly love and for making me believe I am beautiful on the inside and outside. Many thanks to Christine for reading each chapter followed by hour long discussions about the topics which included listening to me ramble on about my passion for ending abuse.

Special thanks to Holly Hudson, Charles Levin and Lily Drew at Munn Avenue Press, Jeanne Hamburg, and Melody Yazdani for outstanding professional services.

My four wonderful children. Each of them add to my life and bring me immense joy. They have taught me more about life than I have ever taught them and much of their knowledge is written into the pages of this book. They are responsible for lighting a fire deep within me to make this world a better place. I found my "why" in life because of them. Mom is the best title in my world and I am honored to be their mother.

To the One who blessed me with strength and made it all possible, thank you for the heavy knock on my shoulder years ago.

www.ingramcontent.com/pod-product-compliance
Lightning Source LLC
Chambersburg PA
CBHW051535120626
46551CB00012B/1239